Invisible Heart

Finding God's Heart

For Ida –
Wishing you all the best.
From my heart to yours
Blessings –
Mary

Mary Emerson

ISBN 978-1-64114-601-2 (Paperback)
ISBN 978-1-64114-602-9 (Digital)

Copyright © 2017 by Mary Emerson
All rights reserved. No part of this publication may be reproduced, distributed, or transmitted in any form or by any means, including photocopying, recording, or other electronic or mechanical methods without the prior written permission of the publisher. For permission requests, solicit the publisher via the address below.

Christian Faith Publishing, Inc.
296 Chestnut Street
Meadville, PA 16335
www.christianfaithpublishing.com

"A Tap at the Window" by Mary Emerson originally appeared in Guideposts magazine and is adapted with permission from the publisher. Copyright © 2014 by Guideposts. All rights reserved.

Printed in the United States of America

Foreword

By
Kay Root

Accepting my sister as a serious writer is a bit like Jesus' childhood friends accepting him as the Son of God, Savior of the world, King of Kings and Lord of Lords. It has taken a little getting used to. So when Mary told me she was writing a book and asked me to read a few of her stories, I thought I would sacrifice some time and appease her. I was impressed—really impressed. The stories were easy to read, tales that everyone could relate to. She managed to weave her faith and Bible verses into her stories. Remembering Bible verses is not my strong suit.

I offered to use my rusty proofreading skills to help my sister polish up her manuscript in the final stages before the book was published. We labored over punctuation. I read the book once, then proofread it again. Seldom did we talk about her words. In two stories, I changed the word *gifts* to *gives*, only to discover what a rich word *gifts* is.

She uses words in her stories that makes one feel like they are right there with her. Oh wait, I was there. I can see the slide she was afraid to go down. And in the story "Grandma's Dish," I see Grandma's bathroom and picture my sister as a little girl. Grandma's laughter still echoes in my memory.

For you the reader, you will catch a glimpse of your own childhood and the memories of times spent with loved ones. I hope you will read these stories to your children or grandchildren, then share the special memories of your life with them.

I love the way Mary tied her experiences to Bible verses. She was always good at that. Back when I was having boyfriend problems in junior high school, Mary wrote a five-page letter to me, connecting my anguish and God's Word. It may have been too much for a young girl who just wanted to stay in her bedroom and cry. I don't remember what my sister said to me, nor the Bible verses she used. What I do remember is the time she took "for me,"-----her little red-headed sister.

There should be someone famous writing the foreward to "Invisible Heart." That person would tell you about the entertaining and heartfelt stories you are about to read. But I can tell you how precious Mary is as a person and sister.

Mary, I am so proud of you---for all that you have become, for your unending faith and your incredible story-telling gift. Maybe one day, you will tell all of us your faith-walk story.

Preface

Perhaps it would have been better had I written about the *darkness* in my life that led to the *light*, first. Yet, when I started writing this book, it was with the intention of sharing short, easy to read stories that would be entertaining or touching: stories that every person could relate to.

A very dear friend of mine pointed out that the *Introduction* to my book has nothing to do with the actual content. Truth be told, the darkness that enveloped my life for so many years, is buried far in my past. It is a world that is now foreign to me, and not a place that I visit very often. Someday, perhaps, I will find the courage to resurrect that part of my life and put it into words.

Even though I have successfully put the *horse before the cart*, I have chosen to leave the *Introduction* as is, so that the reader can catch a glimpse of the path that led me to turn the shipwreck of my life over to a forgiving and merciful Savior.

The book reflects the joy that is the result of that journey.

Introduction

"God uses broken things. It takes broken soil to produce a crop, broken clouds to give rain, broken grain to give bread, broken bread to give strength. It is the broken alabaster box that gives forth perfume.... It is Peter, weeping bitterly, who returns to greater power than ever." (Vance Havener)

Most of us don't arrive at the cross in pristine condition. By the time I reached Golgotha, I was exhausted with hopelessness, and weary of a life that selfishness and bitterness had destroyed.

Even though I believed in God all my life, I didn't know God. One day, spiritually bankrupt and drowning in darkness, I crawled to the foot of the cross and begged for answers. Christ reached down and pulled me into the light.

I was grateful, and I would show God my appreciation for all that he had done for me. I went to all the available Bible studies and belonged to every Christian woman's group in Fargo. I was in charge of our bookstore at church. Every Christian event found me there, front row and center. Those who had known Christ longer than I had were revered and worshipped. The answers to my life came from them. The only one who seemed to be eating the dust as I sped along with my newfound happiness, was God. I said that I knew him. But at the end of the day, I didn't have a clue who he was. There was no time to get to know him, because I was so busy being a successful Christian.

Sometimes, God doesn't say things very nicely. For months, he had been suggesting to me that I might want to spend some time with him. But with a deft wave of my hand, I brushed him off and went on with the task of being wonderful.

Finally, God had enough of me, and the suggesting was over. I don't remember the first time he yelled at me about stopping my endless flurry of activity, but I certainly remember the second and final time when he made it abundantly clear that it was his way, or he would never bother me again. That didn't mean I couldn't come to him. I believe he was weary of trying to get my attention for years.

God commanded me to "stop" everything. With my tail tucked firmly between my legs, humiliated, I pulled myself out of all my involvements. I quit going to the church that I had decided to go to because it was a wonderful church. Certainly God would be happy that I had chosen to be there. He wasn't. He wasn't happy with anything I was doing. The "important" role of bookstore manager was eliminated from my life. Every Bible study was shelved. I was stripped of everything that had become my life, or had it become my god? I returned to my Father, empty and sad. God was still seething.

Parking my body on my knees in front of my bed, I wondered how anyone would be able to see what a wonderful Christian I was when I wasn't allowed to go to any of my "old familiar places." For weeks, I tried to approach God, but he was nowhere to be found. At least he was nowhere where I could find him. I prayed, and I pleaded for his presence. But day after day, all I felt was emptiness.

After weeks of being on my knees, alone, I finally said to God, "I don't care if you never speak to me again. I don't blame you for being angry. But I am not moving away from here, ever, even if you never show up."

That was the moment when my journey to know God began.

Only when I came to the end of myself did God begin to mold me into the person he wanted me to be. On that day, and in that moment, I felt the warmth of God's Spirit bathe me with his love. Suddenly, it didn't matter what the people in my prayer groups thought of me or whether the people in my church admired and respected me. There was a new dawning in my soul, and for the first time in my life, I was truly free.

God taught me how to find his face and how to hear his words with my heart. He assured me of his unconditional love for me. But he also wanted me to know that friendship is a two-way street. He wanted me to care about him, too. He shared his heartaches and injuries with me, and I listened. Through our relationship, I discovered his quirky sense of humor. As in any relationship, we are friends. We know each other well, and we care deeply for each other.

My hope and prayer is that this book will bless you, bring to you a smile, or perhaps a tear. May you be inspired to seek with the special heart that God has given only to you, to join your heart with the invisible heart that belongs to him.

Catch Me, Dad

"I will never leave thee nor forsake thee." (Hebrews 13:5)

For those of us who live in the plains, severe weather doesn't often have a chance to sneak up and nail us. There are no hills or mountains to hide an impending storm. However, several years ago while driving home on a busy four-lane road, the skies turned ominously black. There were no gentle raindrops to announce an oncoming monsoon. Without warning, the heavens opened, and water gushed everywhere. Torrential rains blinded me to anything beyond my steering wheel. The windshield wipers mirrored the terror I was feeling as they slammed furiously back and forth, to no avail.

Until that moment, I was confident that when the time came for me to meet my Maker I would face him bravely and graciously. Yet with the possibility of death being an immediate reality, I had to admit that I was afraid to die.

"Do you remember the day when you climbed to the top of the slide in the park and you were too scared to come down?" God whispered calmly to me.

"Excuse me!" I shot back at him. "I am about to meet you in person here, and you want me to remember something that happened when I was three years old? Maybe we could talk about this another time." I exclaimed frantically.

Yet as I stretched my neck back and forth across the steering wheel, still thinking there was a chance of finding an inch of windshield that I could actually see out of, the memory of sitting on top of that slide was as clear to me as if it were yesterday.

Every year, my grandmother's family met for a reunion in a park central to her relatives. It was post World War II, and material items were in short supply. However, the park where we gathered had an array of playground equipment that was a little piece of heaven for any child. Flitting from one ride to another, I tried to touch the sky with my tippy toes as the swing carried me back and forth. I rode the merry-go-round while the older children pushed to make it go faster and faster until I couldn't catch my breath. My cousins and I rode the teeter-totter together; an extra cousin sat behind me for needed weight. And still, there was more.

On the far side of the playground, a shiny, silver slide gleamed brilliantly in the sunlight, beckoning to me to make it my next adventure. As fast as I could, I ran to the slide and sprang up the steps. It was only when I reached the summit of that magical toy that I realized the ground was miles below me, and I was terrified. Not to worry. My father, my knight in shining armor, would rescue me.

For a little girl, I had a piercing scream—well practiced, I might add. Not only did the shrieks from the top of the slide summon my father, but the horizon looked like a stampede was taking place as half of the picnickers in the park bounded anxiously in my direction. Panicked expressions rapidly dissolved into amused smiles as they assessed the problem at hand. Their humor did little to quell my anxiety. Surely my father would gather me up in his arms and set me safely on solid ground.

He didn't. Instead, he stood at the bottom of the downward-guided missile, with his hands resting firmly on his hips. He seemed totally oblivious to my desperate situation.

Dad encouraged me take my hands off the sides of the slide and let go. He would catch me. He promised. I didn't think so. By now, the eager onlookers, drawn into the melodrama between father and daughter, surrounded the slide to see how this waiting game would play out; their curiosity tweaked as they wondered who would give in first, my father or me. As if he needed any encouragement, the audience seemed to strengthen my father's resolve.

My heart pounded frantically, and embarrassing sobs escaped from my throat, but to no avail. It was painfully obvious even to a three-year-old, that no one was going to save me.

"I'll catch you," my father assured me once again with an encouraging smile on his face.

The battle of the wills finally came to a painful conclusion when it became evident to me that I could die on top of that slide, or I could let go and die at the bottom. Either way, I would be dead. So like Popeye pulling his small body up to supergiant-size strength as he met the much-larger bully Brutus, I gathered every ounce of courage available to me and forced my fingers off the glimmering piece of steel that had been my anchor. With complete dread, I did it. I let go.

It was great! The ever-growing audience laughed heartily at the look of pure, unexpected ecstasy radiating from my face as I slid down the slippery slope and into my father's waiting—long-awaiting—arms.

To the tune of laughter flowing from the delighted spectators, I chirped excitedly, "I want to do it again."

A serious monster was born that morning, and my father paid dearly for his stubbornness. He spent the day catching me as I repeated the thrill over and over, until we were both completely exhausted.

As I finished replaying the scenario through my mind, I noticed that the landscape had appeared once again. The wind had brushed the ominous storm clouds out of harm's way, and where there had been giant threatening thunderheads, the sun reappeared. Against the pitch-black backdrop of the still-dark eastern sky, was a brilliantly colored rainbow arched spectacularly above the city.

"It will be like the day in the park with your father," God whispered. "On the day that you leave this earth, I'll be waiting for you with a smile on my face, arms open wide, ready to catch you."

A Patient's Prayer

"I will never leave thee nor forsake thee." (Hebrews 13:5)

Quietly, I slipped out of the hospital room. The staff needed space to treat my cousin's husband for a serious head injury. And even though I knew that my presence and support were welcome, Tony and his family deserved their privacy.

Wandering aimlessly through the hospital lobby, I noticed a wooden rack hanging prominently on one of the walls. In its frame were copies of prayers that were written by people of many different religions. Curiously, I paged through several of the pamphlets, until I came to this beautiful prayer penned by a person of the Jewish faith. With touching sensitivity and insight, the anonymous author humbly, but brilliantly, snatched the feelings and echoed the words of those who were dealing with illness or injury:

Eternal God, source of healing, out of my distress I call upon you.
Help me to sense your presence at this difficult time.
You have already sent me the gifts of your goodness: the skill of my physician, the concern of others who are helping me.
The compassion of those I love.
I pray that I may be worthy of all these, today and in the days to come.

INVISIBLE HEART

Help me to banish all bitterness; let not despair overcome me.
Grant me patience when the hours are heavy.
Give me courage whenever there is hurt or disappointment.
Keep me trustful in Your love, O God. Give me strength for today and hope for tomorrow.
To Your loving hands I commit my spirit—when asleep and when awake.
You are with me; I shall not fear. Help me, O God, in my time of need.

From the Mouths of Babes

"And their sins and iniquities, I will remember no more." (Hebrews 10:17)

My friend Robin was in charge of a group of six-year-old children for her church's vacation Bible school program, while caring for her granddaughter at the same time. Even though Cerena was younger than the other children, she loved joining in with the class, making crafts and listening to the Bible stories.

I remember the first time I saw Cerena. Her ebony-black, naturally curly hair fell into long ringlets that ended at her shoulders, contrasting her flawless, milky-white skin. She looked like a delicate porcelain doll. It was her eyes that changed that image. One look at her steely blue eyes told you that there was no nonsense about this child. She was all business.

After teaching the lesson, Robin gathered her youngsters around her and demonstrated the chosen craft for the day. All was quiet as the children busied themselves with their projects. It was Cerena who broke the silence by deciding to teach a lesson of her own.

"My sister hit me on the cheek," Cerena said firmly. "And it hurt. And I was mad at her, and I didn't want to forgive her. And I told God, 'I don't want to forgive Cierra for hurting me.' And I had to ask God to help me forgive my sister."

Out of the mouths of babes.

Several years ago, my cousin's husband stumbled out of their house and into the arms of another woman. The timing couldn't have been worse. Their teenage son was going through an emotionally difficult time, and the couple had financed much of what they owned to get help for him. Not only did the husband's departure devastate his family emotionally, but the financial strain was staggering.

My cousin was my friend, and watching her life crumble was like watching a brilliant piece of crystal fall from a shelf, shattering into a million pieces right in front of my eyes. Not only did *Jim* leave *Gail*, but the congregation that *Gail* had ministered to for years booted her out of their church and onto the street with no thanks for all she had personally sacrificed for them. *Gail* was now a divorcee, and at a time when she desperately needed support, her congregation no longer had any use for her. Not only was *Gail* my cousin, but she was my friend. How much more could she possibly endure? If a heart could cry, my heart sobbed for her.

Christ requires a couple of things from us, and forgiveness is a given. There is no debating with God on that point. I thought about how much God had forgiven me, yet I was sorely injured for someone I dearly loved. If I forgave *Jim*, wouldn't I also be joining the group of people who had betrayed my cousin? I had no power to make her life better. The only thing I had to offer her was a shoulder to cry on, my friendship, and my prayers.

Quietly, like a burglar sneaking around a house in the middle of the night so as not to be caught, I tucked that little piece of unforgiveness into a far corner of my heart, thinking surely God would never find it there. Wrong.

It's funny, isn't it? It's funny how one seemingly insignificant seed planted in an invisible, unused part of our heart, can grow into a huge, hideous weed without us ever noticing that a monster is subtly taking over our whole heart. Because that little piece of unforgiveness toward *Jim* made it a little easier to justify not forgiving the next person who injured me, or someone I loved.

I had some housecleaning to do. And like Cerena, I had to ask God for his help.

Good-bye, Mighty Angel of Light

"How art though fallen from heaven, O Lucifer?" (Isaiah 14:12)

A long time ago, there was in God's kingdom a most magnificent angel. His name was Lucifer. Of all the angels who dwelled and worked with God, who loved and were loved by God, Lucifer was the closest to the Master. His closeness to God gave him such radiance that he became the brightest angel of all the angels in God's realm. This is the story of Satan, who went from being an angel of light to an angel of darkness.

Some questions are very difficult to put to God. Yet over the years, I have ever been surprised by his clear and straightforward answers. Forging on where angels fear to tread, I slowly and softly approached him one day concerning the subject of Lucifer.

"It is so hard to lose someone you love," I said with my eyes downcast. "Was it ... well, you know. He was so close to you. Were you devastated when the friendship between you and Lucifer ended?"

There was a long pause—then God spoke.

"He was the brightest of all the creatures in heaven," God said. "I loved him above all the other angels. Do you want to know what happened?" His voice was so soft, so full of pain, that my heart ached for him. I wondered if it would have been kinder to drop the subject, but by now, I was entranced.

"Yes," I almost whispered. "Please."

"Do you know how he got to be the brightest angel?"

I didn't.

"He loved me more than any of the other angels in heaven loved me. That is how he became so brilliant. The closer anything is to me, the brighter it becomes. One day, Lucifer noticed that the other angels around him were not as light as he was, and he became critical of them. Pride was born.

"I reminded him that I was a God of mercy, and that in order to be with me, he had to be merciful too. He refused. Disobedience was born. There was no room in heaven for two rulers with such opposite ideas. He started to move away from me into another realm. The farther away from me he went, the darker he became, until there was no light left in him at all."

"This is how Satan went from being the brightest, most radiant angel in heaven, to the darkest, most evil angel that there has ever been."

Grandma's Dish

"In thy presences is fullness of joy." (Psalm 16:11)

There are certain things that happen in our lives from which we never recover. A gorgeous spring day spent with my grandmother Brown provided such an experience.

My grandmother lived a few short blocks from us when I was growing up in the small town of Warren, Minnesota. After a long winter, the windows in her house were open, and a soft breeze gently pushed the curtains back and forth, filling the air with the fresh smell of spring. I suppose that I must have been about four years old at the time. My mother had left me in the care of my grandmother for the afternoon, and as usual, I was shadowing her every step, chatting endlessly, no doubt. So when grandmother made a trip to the bathroom, without missing a beat, I simply followed her.

Grandmother's house was very tiny, the bathroom about the size of a small closet. There was a small tub on one side of the little room. Across from the tub and next to the door stood a sink with the stool positioned between the sink and the window. As Grandmother and I continued our visit—she on the throne and me sitting directly across from her on the edge of the tub, my hands folded neatly in my lap—something happened that changed my life forever.

Before I go on to explain the unfortunate incident, you must understand a little bit about my grandmother. Although she and my grandfather had very little money, she was raised in a well-to-do, prominent family. Tall for that time, Grandmother was stately, regal, poised, always careful to maintain her dignity. Her posture was enviable. She was a well-bred lady.

Now it is time to get to the bones of the matter. As we conversed, Grandmother turned her head slightly toward the door, and that was when it happened. She sneezed.

Suddenly, right in front of me, her teeth flew out of her mouth, across the bathroom floor, and came to a screeching halt at the base of the door. Had the bathroom door not been closed, God only knows how far those teeth would have traveled.

No one had ever explained to me that there were people who could remove their teeth. My eyes, wider than usual, darted from my grandmother's teeth, now resting comfortably on the bathroom floor, to my grandmother's face. No doubt Grandmother sympathized with the child sitting across from her, in shock to the point of being catatonic. But try as she might, she was not able to compose herself. Stately grandmother, proper grandmother, was now bent over with her face in her hands, trying unsuccessfully to squelch the laughter leaking uncontrollably from some place deep inside of her.

As for me, I could barely manage so much as a whisper as I asked her what had just happened. Understand, I was pretty sure that my grandmother had just lost her teeth forever, and I was feeling horrible for her.

"That's my plate," Grandmother explained as she struggled to regain her composure. Adding to my anguish, she asked me to retrieve her teeth and return them to her.

My exact reply doesn't immediately come to mind. But I remember what I was thinking: *Not for all the money in the world.*

I slithered carefully along the edge of the bathtub and out of the bathroom, avoiding as best I could the "interesting" item lying by the door. My aunt Loretta happened to be standing in the adjoining room as I emerged. My now-almost-critical condition did not go unnoticed.

"What's the matter, dear?" Aunt Loretta asked with genuine concern.

"Grandma blew her dish," I stated with a look of total bewilderment.

Somehow, I was not managing to successfully convey the severity of the event that I had just witnessed. Aunt Loretta could not contain her laughter. And when my mother came to pick me up, upon hearing the story, she dissolved into laughter too. Sometimes, adults are absolutely no help at all.

As for me, I was careful not to sneeze for a very long time.

Here We Go Again

"The Lord giveth and the Lord taketh away; blessed be the name of the Lord." (Job 1:21)

I sighed and took a deep breath as my eyes fell on the book of Job. It is the one book in the Bible that irks me. No, it's more than that. This book *infuriates* me every time I read it. "*How* can you let all of these horrible things happen to Job? How in the end can you *yell* at Job when he has been loyal to you no matter *what* has happened to him? *How* can you leave him *alone* for so *long* as he begs for, no, *pleads* for understanding?" I would rant. The palms of my hands jerk upward in a gesture that says, "*What the heck?*"

I know. I know that God is right. But frankly, Job's situation could be our situation. I sucked it up and began to read the book of Job. First of all, Job loses all of his belongings. Then all of his children die. How would we feel if that happened to us?

To top everything off, God disappears from Job. To me that is the scariest part of all. Where do we go when the only person we know who has the power to help us when we need help, abandons us? The first chapter isn't over, and already I'm seething. I know it's not a good thing to be angry at God. Still, isn't lying to God worse? Reluctantly, I carry on. Maybe as I journey through the Bible, it would just be better to avoid this book altogether.

I don't. I sigh. And continue to read the book of Job.

Poor Job, who has never done anything but good to his friends and family, loved his God and served him, finds himself covered from one end of his body to the other with boils. Imagine. And if that weren't bad enough, Job's buddies, his best friends, pummel him with accusations about how he has failed and wronged God, because surely God wouldn't allow these things to happen to a just man.

I come to the part in the book where God wants to know why Job thinks he knows better than God does. By now, my temper is equal to the whirlwind that the Lord is speaking to Job through.

"Where were you when I laid the foundations of the earth?" God asks Job. "Where were you when I made the seas or the stars in the heavens?"

Where is the correlation? I wonder.

Then unexpectedly, I heard Christ's voice say, "You hurt my dad."

The breath was almost sucked out of me. I? Me? I had the power to injure someone I loved so very much but quite frankly was pretty ticked off at, as I knew I would be before I read the first word in the book of Job.

The next day as I was spending time with my Father, I humbly apologized to him. "It's just that I don't understand this book," I said sadly. "The book of Job defeats me, even before I start reading it."

And so God kindly and patiently explained a few things to me. "I wanted—I *needed* to know that there was someone on earth that I could trust, no matter what. I wanted to know that there was someone who would be loyal to me despite great adversity. I wanted someone to understand my frustrations and hurts, too. Through his anguish he remained my friend: my loyal friend.

Color me speechless.

God said that a thousand years are as a day to him. When we can't locate our Heavenly Father, a day seems like a thousand years to us. God tells us not to lean on our own understanding, and here is a perfect example why. He gives us so much. Perhaps we can't begrudge God if he wants and needs something back for himself.

From God's Heart to Ours

"Come near before the Lord, for he hath heard your murmurings." (Exodus 16:9)

The hardcover book with a picture of two little girls tucked snuggly into a canopied bed, covered with a fluffy patchwork quilt, was a gift given to me as a little child by my stately, proper, and always kindly grandmother: and my charming, but not-so-proper and often-irreverent maiden aunt. Between the book covers were stories from the Bible and lessons taught to children by their parents and friends about sharing, obeying, and loving.

There were tales about the brave king David standing up to the towering Goliath, and the little boy Samuel who heard God calling to him in the middle of the night.

It was with no small amount of indignation that I had missed the boat by several thousand years. God didn't call my name in the middle of the night. What made Samuel so much more special to God than I was, excuse me very much? And why couldn't I have lived when Jesus did? The day of miracles had long passed, and I had missed seeing them. How much fun would it have been to watch Jesus turn two fishes and five loaves of bread into enough food to feed thousands of people? Truth be told, I just hate missing out on anything.

Of course, as a child, it never occurred to me that life might not have been so easy back in Christ's time. Transportation consisted of hoofing it, or sitting on the back of a sassy mule, eating the dirt kicked up on the rough and rugged road by the clomping hoofs from an often-stubborn beast of burden. No electric blanket? No electric anything for another 1,900 years. Perhaps being born in the twentieth century wasn't so bad after all. Still, I hungered for a personal touch that God seemed to bestow on certain people in biblical times.

Today, I have come to learn that God is still the God of miracles. He still speaks to us, answers our prayers, keeps his promises, and surprises us with his presence when we are not expecting him.

Sometimes, I wish that my mother and my father could come back just for a day, even for an hour. I would apologize to them for being a stubborn, self-centered, ungrateful child. I was. Most people who knew me as a teenager would say, "There is no hope for that young lady. Dispose of her." But God, who is love, sends a piece of his heart to each child that he creates. No matter how out of control our lives might become on our journey through this world, God never gives up on anyone. He never stops hoping that someday, the gift of love from his heart to our heart, will be returned to him with the words, *I love you back.*

Just Start

"And the ark rested in the seventh month, on the seventeenth day of the month, upon the mountains of Ararat." (Genesis: 8:4)

The thought of Noah's ark parked somewhere on the mountain Ararat has always fascinated me. What is so compelling about discovering something concrete concerning God? Wouldn't it be fun to hike the peaks of those mountains, search their deep crevices, and be the one to discover the vessel that for weeks cradled God's creation safely through stormy waters? How amazing would it be to touch and see the incredible ship commissioned by God? Much of Ararat is encased in ice, snow, and glaciers. Since I don't like heights, and I certainly hate being cold, this dream is the perfect example of how anticipation can be far better than reality.

Errol Cummings was an explorer who made many expeditions to Turkey in search of Noah's ark, where Mt. Ararat majestically stands. Finding the ancient vessel was his passion. But as Mr. Cummings grew older, he reluctantly abandoned his lifelong dream of ever discovering the boat. Errol's wife, Violet, chronicled his journeys to the mountain in the book *The Search for Noah's Ark*.

One day, a young man knocked on the door of the Cummings home, and asked to speak to Errol. Mrs. Cummings explained that he wasn't there, but she inquired of the young person standing before her if there might be something she could do for him. With great excitement, the visitor shared that he was going to Turkey to look for

Noah's ark, and he wanted Errol's advice on how to go about searching for the vessel.

Violet's simple answer was profound and memorable.

"Start." Violet instructed wisely. "Just start. Because if you don't take that first step, you will never find the ark."

As a person who is easily overwhelmed, Violet's practical wisdom rings daily in my ears. If we ever want to accomplish anything, we have to take that first step.

Invisible Heart

"Yet in my flesh shall I see God." (Job 16:26)

My mother and I were standing in the dining room of our tiny cracker box of a house when I asked her, "Where is my heart, Mom?"

Tenderly, she picked up my little four-year-old hand and placed it over my heart. I still remember the first time I felt the gentle fluttering in my chest. "Do you have a heart?" My mother smiled and explained that everyone has a heart: that they couldn't live without one.

Actually, each one of us has two hearts: the physical heart that powers our body and an invisible heart that powers our soul. Unlike the first heart, the invisible heart has never been seen by the eyes of man. It has never been dissected in a lab, never held in the hands of a doctor or a scientist. Made especially for you, this one-of-a-kind heart can only be held in the hands of God. Only God can follow the beating path of this heart that leads to an unseen place somewhere deep within us that houses our soul. God alone has the power to soar with us to the highest point of heaven or descend anxiously beside us if we sink to a place of despair and hopelessness.

Our eyes are physically limited by what they are able to see, our mouths sadly inadequate to express our deepest feelings. Our ears are not capable of hearing every spoken word. But this mysterious heart gifted to each of us is not bound by our physical bodies.

Sometimes, the passion or sentiment of a person's invisible heart can fill the whole universe. God created this heart so that we are able to see the unseen and hear God's voice.

There is a secret door hidden in our invisible heart. The latch is located on our side, and Christ, ever a gentleman, never enters into this unseen personal place unwanted or uninvited. The power to open this door and share our heart with him is ours alone.

God has an invisible heart too. This heart is where he holds your soul and his unconditional love for you. Together, these hearts join to create an intimate space that makes you a one of a kind, like no other person, special to God. It is a place reserved for just the two of you.

Little Church Mice

"I was glad when they said unto me, let us go into the house of the Lord." (Psalm 122:1)

We belong to a lovely beige-stoned Presbyterian Church, nestled snugly among magnificent giant elms and positioned squarely in the middle of downtown Fargo, North Dakota. The stately old edifice has stood in its comfortable resting place, sleepily watching endless changes to the city since before the turn of the twentieth century. The beautiful walls of this statuesque building houses its faithful and devoted parishioners, many of whom have attended church there for most of, if not all, their lives.

One morning, as the eleven o'clock services were about to begin, a very humble-looking young couple drifted cautiously into the church sanctuary. Cradled softly in the woman's arms was a newborn baby boy. The couple, who appeared to be in their late teens, scanned the well-attired congregation. I watched as their countenance fell. It was apparent from the stricken look on their youthful faces that they felt painfully out of place as they slowly made their way to a pew directly in front of me.

My heart ached for them as I struggled, virtually uninspired, to think of some way to make them feel welcome and at ease. No one should feel uncomfortable in any church, but this young couple looked like a family of stricken church mice who had accidentally fallen through a hidden trapdoor in the rafters, with no hope of escaping.

The young father stood nervously erect, much resembling a wooden toy soldier. His face was gaunt and expressionless, except for the sudden fierce look of protection evident from behind his silver-framed, wire-rimmed spectacles. He carried himself with a quiet air of dignity on a slight frame that appeared to shoulder a weight far beyond his years. His unimaginably thin, tan jacket didn't stand a fighting chance against our frigid, northern winters.

No words were ever exchanged between the young couple. I never saw them look directly at each other. Yet there seemed to be a silent communication and understanding between them that surpassed any words that could be spoken. Their love for each other and their son was unmistakable. The focus of these two almost children was directed toward their newborn baby, as together they gazed down at him.

Quiet, and a great deal shorter than her husband, the plump young mother, with a totally blank look on her face, moved sheepishly toward her husband until she was so close to him that their arms appeared to be fused together. Her full, round cheeks blazed rosy red, contrasted by bright, blue eyes that protruded just slightly from beneath their lids. Short, blond, curly hair cropped in tight curls close to her scalp overstated the roundness of her ruddy face. She stayed bundled up throughout the service in her worn, gray down coat.

A set of bright, blue eyes gazed up at his worshipping parents. It was as if this child knew that—for this time in his life, at least, they were his world. His little blue sleeper was covered with those little *nubby* things that appear after several trips to the washing machine, leading me to believe that his outfit had probably been worn many times by another baby before this child was even born.

Instantly, I wished that my clothing were a little less nice. From the expressions on the young couple's strained faces, I suspect they wished for the same thing in reverse. The congregation began to take notice of the uncomfortable youngsters, who seemed as trapped as a chicken in a cage, about to be featured for Sunday dinner.

Our pastor and assistant pastor, outfitted in their flowing white robes and with their smiling Sunday faces, were seated on the ornate wooden bench that faced the congregation. The choir briskly made their way down the center aisle from the back of the sanctuary to the front of the church, their long black robes swishing softly as they passed between the wooden pews. The processional hymn filled the place of worship with melodious voices of praise. Upon reaching the altar, they split to the right or left, ascending several steps to the choir loft, meeting once again in the middle of three rows of pews, each row higher than the other. Taking their places as they finished the hymn, they faced the congregation and remained standing for the opening prayer.

Huge golden pipes from the church's pristine organ rose majestically behind them, the shortest beginning on either side of the choir loft to the tallest pipe located almost ceiling height in the middle. The dark wood podium used for reading the scriptures and delivering the morning sermon stood alone to the left of the altar, while a huge bouquet of colorful, beautifully arranged flowers rested on the opposite side, sitting gracefully on a stand reserved for just that purpose.

Perhaps the most striking and infinitely beautiful part of the church is the finely detailed stained glass windows lining both sides of the sanctuary. Streams of morning sunlight poured through the colored glass, magnifying pictures of Jesus and his apostles.

While most of the congregation was focused with varying degrees of interest on the service, I was too involved with the situation unfolding in front of me to notice much else. As I sat quietly, it occurred to me that this little family was not altogether unlike Joseph, Mary, and baby Jesus.

From many accounts, Mary and Joseph were in their middle teens when they were entrusted by God with the overwhelming task of caring for and raising his son. Not only were they young, but Mary and Joseph were probably fairly poor. Had Joseph, Mary, and baby Jesus shown up one morning at our church, fresh out of their stable dwelling, would we have greeted them warmly, invited them to share our comfortable, richly padded velvet pews, or would we have treated them with kindly indifference? Just how different was this young, poor couple in their circumstances than Mary and Joseph had been in theirs?

The service seemed to draw on for an eternity as I impatiently awaited its end. My mind was made up. I would take the hands of these young parents and assure them that we were pleased that they had chosen to visit our church. I would extend an invitation to them to return the next week. Undoubtedly, others would contribute to dissolving their discomfort at the close of the service too. But as I slowly lifted my chin from my chest, unfolded my hands, and opened my eyes after the final prayer, they were nowhere to be seen.

"Come, Come, Ye Saints" bellowed from the monstrous golden pipes of the church's organ, heaving beautiful notes that connected like flowing dots dancing freely along an invisible line. I bolted out of the front door, hoping to head off the little trio before they could make their getaway. But it was too late. As surely as a gunslinger heading out of Dodge, grateful to do so with his life, all that was left to be seen of the elusive visitors was the back end of an old, rusty, red pickup rumbling west on Second Avenue, leaving in its wake small, round gray-and-blue puffs of smoky exhaust.

With little hope, I scanned the sanctuary every Sunday morning for weeks, looking for the young couple and their sweet little boy. In my heart, I knew it was a futile search. Yet hardly a Sunday goes by without thoughts of the morning they had visited our church and unknowingly touched my heart. I never saw them again.

Which Way Did That Star Go?

"And lo, the star, which they saw in the east, went before them, till it came and stood over where the young child was." (Matthew 2:9)

We were living in St. Louis, and the only thing that I dreaded more than going out in the stifling July heat was rush-hour traffic. Being an accomplished procrastinator, my errands had been left undone, again, and we were critically low on everything. My hand was on the doorknob that led to the garage when I heard God say, *You haven't read your devotions today*.

His request brought back memories of my childhood. It seemed that whenever I was about to run out the back door to play with my friends, my mother would inevitably call me back to complete some unfinished chore. If she was out of sight, I would quietly turn the doorknob and sneak out of the house before she could stop me.

I'll do my devotions when I get back home, I promised, wondering why it could possibly matter to God when I did them.

Still, God insisted that I not leave the house until the task was finished, and in that moment, I knew that a get-away was not going to happen.

With little enthusiasm, I plopped down on our bed and rested my Bible in the crook of my folded legs. I opened the book to the place where I had left off reading the previous day: Matthew 2. The story of the Magi.

I know this story. This will only take a moment, I thought smugly. *I can still get my errands done before every person in St. Louis is on their way home from work.*

Dashing through the chapter with the speed of a well-heeled racehorse, barn door in sight, I was feeling quite pleased with myself. We were in the home stretch—until God stopped me at the ninth verse.

"Read that verse again," God instructed.

"I've read this verse a million times!" I exclaimed. "I've known this story since I was a small child."

"Read it again," he insisted.

With a huge sigh of resignation, I reluctantly read the verse one more time. *And lo, the star which they saw in the east went before them.*

My hands flew up in exasperation, and with a quizzical expression on my face, I said, *"So?"*

Why does God bother with me?

"Mary. What in the universe moves to the east? The sun moves from the east to the west, so does the moon. Nothing in the sky moves in an easterly direction. The miracle of the star was not its brightness. The miracle that caught the attention of the Magi was that the star was traveling in an impossible direction. It was my way of announcing to the world that at the birth of my Son, everything would change."

And so it did. The law was now covered by mercy.

I don't remember if I made it out of the house that day. It no longer seemed to matter. The lesson I learned was that God is excited about his mysteries, and he loves to share his mysterious ways with each one of us.

Living, Breathing God

"God that made the world and all things therein, seeing that he is Lord of heaven and earth, dwelleth not in temples made with hands." (Acts 17:24)

I was sitting in the driveway at my friend Robin's house, waiting for her to come out to my car so that we could spend some time alone together. When it comes to Robin, I often wait. She is seldom on time, which is a small downside to her personality. Robin does things slowly, but she never misses anything. She takes the time to observe everything around her. And when she is with me, she is never in a hurry to move on to something or someone else. She gifts all the time in the world to our friendship. We are polar opposites, Robin and I, which is probably one of the reasons that our friendship has endured for years.

Robin was going through a really rough time, and as I waited for her in my car, which I kept running to keep from freezing to death in the early North Dakota spring, I bowed my head and said a little prayer, that God would watch over her and protect her. If I offered any advice, I wanted it to be God's wisdom, not mine.

As my head was bent, the most unexpected thing happened. I felt Christ's presence directly behind me. And that wasn't all. On the back of my neck where the skin was exposed by my lowered head, I felt Christ's warm breath moving across the skin on my neck.

Living God. Christ resurrected from the dead. It had never occurred to me that Christ had breath in him. Yet unexpectedly from nowhere, Jesus had let me know once again that he was present when I called his name. These are the moments in our relationship that are the treasures we hold dear in our hearts. The unexpected times, those uninvited times, when Christ chooses to share a piece of his wonderment with us.

Lot's Wife

*"But his wife looked back from behind him, and
she became a pillar of salt." (Genesis 19:26)*

Several years ago, my daughter was offered a job as an administrative assistant to an executive at a Minneapolis-based business, in the salt division of their company. The advancement meant that she and her family would have to relocate from Fargo, North Dakota to Minneapolis, Minnesota.

On a warm summer day, I watched as the moving van pulled out of my daughter's driveway, taking Lisa, her husband and our four-year-old grandson to their new home two hundred miles away from us. Much of my heart followed closely behind them.

A few weeks later, I made the trip to Minneapolis for a visit. Lisa was excited to show off her new office. She introduced me to her coworkers and her supervisor: someone who appreciated and adored her. After touring my daughter's new surroundings, Lisa said, "I have one more person I want you to meet. Come with me, Mom." She led me through a maze of desks and out into the lobby.

"I want you to meet Lot's wife."

Directly in front of me was the statue of a lady standing about seven feet tall.

"She's totally made out of salt," my daughter explained with a mischievous smile on her face. "That's why we call her Lot's wife.

Do you see this little chip right here?" She pointed to a small, slight indentation on the upper part of the statue's torso.

I did.

As I slowly ran my hand over the statue that made petrified wood seem softer than marshmallow, Lisa shared the story of Lot's wife's unfortunate encounter.

"One night," Lisa began, "the night watchman was making his rounds to all the floors in the building. As he walked off the elevator in the dark, he spotted Lot's wife standing by the elevator. Thinking she was an intruder, he shot her, and the chip in her chest is where the bullet hit her."

Thankfully, it wasn't a person. Needless to say, the guard was standing in line at the unemployment office the next morning.

Paradise

"Ah Lord God! Behold, thou has made the heaven and the earth by thy great power and stretched out arm, and there is nothing too hard for thee." (Jeremiah 32:7)

Several years ago, my husband was sent to Hawaii on a business trip, and I was invited to go along with him. We pored over glossy posters advertising the islands, as if one needed much convincing. Along with soothing, gentle waves lapping at the sand, beautifully bronzed bodies relaxing on white sandy beaches were also featured on the posters. I was not going to be the one to ruin this perfect paradise. With the determination of a miner searching for gold, I scoured the stores in Fargo for a Hawaiian-looking bathing suit. It didn't take long before I realized that finding a bathing suit in the middle of winter in North Dakota is a daunting task.

Upon arriving in Oahu, we checked into our room, and I couldn't slide into my new floral swimsuit fast enough. With suntan lotion slathered in all the appropriate places, I grabbed a large fluffy white towel from the bathroom, a book bought just for this occasion, my husband, and we headed to the beach. It was time to try out the sunshine, the tropical temperatures, and the promise of rest from the grind of our everyday lives.

Dick and I took ownership of a comfortable spot on a warm piece of Hawaiian sand. Heaven it was. We were surrounded by perfectly tanned people, wading, splashing, and swimming in the magnificent turquoise ocean that lay only feet from where we were lounging. Nearby, children and adults constructed sand castles, some of them quite magnificent.

I slid my sunglasses down from the top of my head and took a deep breath. There were no children who needed to be shuffled from one part of the city to the next. No dirty laundry that needed attending to. No meals that had to be cooked or dogs to be walked. My life, which so seldom belonged to me, was mine for a whole week.

However, without warning, my vision of paradise crumbled. No, it wasn't an unexpected sneaker wave or a tsunami. The disaster was me. Shortly, very shortly after arriving at the beach, I made a horrible discovery. I *hated* just sitting there. I mean, I really hated it, and so did my husband.

Within ten minutes of watching the peaceful ocean and digging our toes into the warm sand, we picked up our towels and books. Still shiny with sun tan lotion, we marched back to our room. Much to our surprise, we discovered something about ourselves, and each other. While lying on a towel soaking in sunshine might be relaxing for most people, it certainly wasn't for us. We spent our holiday golfing and sightseeing. The beach that had been the focus of our trip was viewed from a distance.

We are such activists, aren't we? We always want to be doing something. Yet God invites us to sit. He invites us to sit at his feet. He invites us to be patient: an act that makes me question why he made me such an active nugget of clay. I do know this. When God wants us to spend time with him, it is pure magic. God! The God of heaven and earth wants you to sit quietly before him so that, like a sponge in the ocean, you can soak up all the wonders that he is eager to share with no one else but you.

Leave Me Alone! I'll Do It Myself

"I can of my own self do nothing." (John 5:30)

"Leave me alone! I'll do it myself." There is no doubt in my mind that these were the first words out of my mouth—ever: words that have not always served me well.

Writing has always been my passion. To be honest with you, it's really the only talent I have. When I was younger, I felt like a failure much of the time, because I thought that I should have been good at everything. Certainly, many of my classmates seemed to be. When it came to sports, I was always the last person to be chosen on the school playground, and then to the tune of "Do we have to have her on our team?" What can one do when you have a mutant sports gene? I could run though. Just ask any of my babysitters who tried to catch me at bedtime.

As a young mother, I wrote—a lot. One night, God asked me if writing was more important to me than he was. Most people don't understand this, but I took everything that I had ever written and threw it into the trash can, with the promise to God that I would never write again until he told me to. At that moment, I had an inkling of what Abraham must have felt as he held a knife to his son's throat just before the angel of the Lord stopped him from sacrificing Isaac.

A lot of my heart and soul walked out of my house on that particular garbage day. Still, I knew that it was the right thing to do, even though it wasn't easy to understand his request. God was my first love. I wanted to obey him.

Years went by. Our children grew up and moved away. We moved away too. And finally, I felt God nudging me to write.

If there was one thing that I had confidence in, it was my writing ability. God generously offered to assist me, but I brushed him off with a "Thanks, but no thanks. I'll do it myself." Let me assure you that the Tin Man from the *Wizard of Oz* had nothing on me. *Rusty* doesn't begin to describe my writing skills after they had been sitting in a dusty corner for years. There is a lesson to be learned here. Why did I ever think that I could do anything apart from God?

The words on the pages in front of me were "dead." And no matter how much I tried to breathe life into them, I couldn't stand to read what I had written. How could I expect anyone else to enjoy or be blessed by what I had written? Once again, my writing was shelved.

Whenever I asked God what his will was for me, the answer was always one word: "Write." Still, every time I approached my computer, I did so with a banquet of negative emotions. Fear of failing topped the list. Every day, I walked away from my computer defeated, complete with the assurance that I had let God down—again.

Slowly, humbly, I sank to my knees and confessed to God that I may have had just a little bit of pride concerning my writing, and would he give me another chance? Oh, and would he please help me?

He did. This time, we did the writing together.

Oh! That Is Too Bad

*"The Lord shall fight for you, and ye shall
hold your peace." (Exodus 14:14)*

Our first home was small but cozy. There was a front porch for the children to play on, a living room, a den, the one and only bathroom, a small hallway, and an adorable kitchen with a charming bay window covered by billowy white, Priscilla curtains. Three bedrooms finished off the house on the second level. Every house that we have ever owned has been special. But there seems to be a little more excitement and gratitude when you are able to buy your first home.

Let's just say that for the most part surprises are not usually fun or welcome. Upon opening the door just before moving into our home, it was immediately obvious that the previous owners had stripped the house. I mean, light-switch plates, light bulbs, light fixtures and the mirror off the bathroom wall.

Understand, we were young and poor. Often, I would have to take our empty pop bottles to the grocery store and exchange them for bread or milk. I am not sure why it never occurred to us to visit with our real estate agent about the missing necessities. Instead, we coughed up the money and replaced the items ourselves.

Angry, and feeling very violated, my first reaction was to lash out at the people who had done this to us. But I knew that anger and resentment could destroy a person and, as a Christian, there were two things that I needed to do. First of all, I had to forgive the people who basically robbed us. At least it certainly felt like a robbery had taken place. And the second thing I needed to do was to put my anger and hurt into God's hands and let him take care of the situation. I knew he would. That is his promise to us many times over again. Never in my wildest dreams did I imagine that he would show me how he honored my act of forgiveness and faith in him.

We had been living in our house for about a year when several of my neighbors congregated on our front yard for a visit. During the conversation I overhead one of my friends say, "It certainly was too bad about the *Johnsons'* new home."

My ears sprang into action at the mention of the previous house owner's name.

"What about their new house?" I asked with genuine curiosity.

"Their house was full of cockroaches when they moved into it," piped up the unwitting informant.

Understand that surviving the long and frigid winters in this part of the country can be challenging at times. There are few perks when it comes to our cold weather. However, one advantage is that apart from an occasional field mouse, unwelcome house varmints do not exist in our climate. In all the years that I have lived in this part of the world, never-ever have I heard of one cockroach sneaking into North Dakota.

"Oh. That is too bad," I replied.

While I felt sympathy for the *Johnsons'* sad plight, a little piece of my heart was grinning from ear to ear. God had kept his promise to me. And he managed to do it without my help.

What Makes You Free

"Stand fast therefore in the liberty wherewith Christ hath made us free, and be not entangled again with the yoke of bondage." (Galatians 5:1)

Something that I really look forward to are the occasional questions that my cousin *Gail*, a minister, poses every now and then on Facebook. She loves to fish for ideas and opinions for her upcoming sermons. Not only is it fun to see her thought-provoking questions, but equally as fun are the comments she gets from family, friends, and parishioners.

Last week, *Gail* asked the question, *What makes you free?* Many well-thought-out answers were shared on the site, but the mutual thread among the ideas presented by the readers was that they were free because they did not have to worry about God *getting* them. They knew in their hearts that God loved them for who he created them to be.

The week had been a busy one, and before I could find the time to get to my dryer, the clothes had become a pile of mass destruction. With a sigh, I placed one of my favorite movies into the DVD player and pushed the play button. Ironing is not my favorite job, but at least I would be entertained while doing the tedious task set before me.

The movie I chose was *Miss Potter*. It is the story about the author of *Peter Rabbit* and other famous animated tales. Born into a family of privilege, Beatrix was often lonely, and seldom fit into the social scene of Victorian London that was so vitally critical to her mother. The man who was Beatrix's publisher, and the love of her life, died at a very young age, leaving the young author devastated.

As I observed Beatrix' mother, a woman acutely concerned with whom she knew and how she was perceived by others, God said something that surprised me as much as it rang true:

"She lives in a coffin, don't you think?"

Mrs. Potter was certainly unpleasant. But even more certainly, she was just a sad person. She didn't care about her family's feelings. Her only concern seemed to be how they appeared to those she was desperate to impress. She was dead to everything else. God's words made me wonder how many times I had wanted to impress someone over wanting to please God.

The resounding words, *Free to love Christ, free to be loved by Christ* on *Gail's* Facebook page said it all. God desires that we are not the walking dead, or living our lives in a coffin. Like butterflies, we are free of the confines of a cocoon. Free to love him. Free to know him. Alive because of him.

Eggs, Glorious Eggs

"Blessed are all they that wait for him." (Isaiah 30:18)

"What shall we talk about today?" God gently asked as I trekked along a quiet road to visit my mother.

This question comes up frequently when I am alone with God. Usually, I return the question to him. But this time, I knew exactly what I wanted to talk about.

"I want to understand about the three in one," I replied earnestly. "I want to know how you can be God the Father, God the Son, and God the Holy Spirit. How can the 'three' of you be 'one' of you?"

His immediate answer was, "Eggs."

I smiled. Not because I understood what he was trying to teach me, but because the thought of eggs brought me back to another place, another time.

My father's parents lived on a small farmstead in northern Minnesota. So many precious, lifelong memories were made there. In the summertime, I was often awakened by a strutting, crowing rooster, who made it his mission in life to sound off right under my bedroom window in the early hours of the morning, long before I was ready to get out of bed.

In the winter, breakfast consisted of hot oatmeal topped with brown sugar and fresh cream brought in from the barn by my grandfather. There was always an assortment of farmyard animals: baby kitties, and docile, curious cows grazing in the fields. Fluffy white lambs taught us the biblical lesson as to why we were often compared to sheep. On many occasions, Skippy, the sheepdog, would accompany us on a search-and-rescue mission as we tried to track down the wayward critters, who never seemed to have a clue that they were lost and in possible danger.

The most abundant animals that belonged to my grandparents were chickens. Their eggs were supposed to be deposited in the henhouse. But sometimes, or often, the chickens didn't get the memo. Twice a day, my grandmother would pick up her wire basket and scour the property for the delicate oval treasures that had missed their mark. Every egg she found added to her spending money, which was her only source of personal income.

For just a moment, I would love to be standing in her kitchen again, warmed by the fire in the old cookstove. Once more, I would love to watch Grandma remove her "everyday" apron and hang it next to the "fancy" one, which was available at a second's notice in case unexpected company arrived. I loved to watch as she tied her wool scarf under her chin—or several chins—when the weather was cool: my eyes following this beloved woman as she walked out the door to hunt for the elusive eggs.

"Think about it, Mary," God said as he coaxed me back to the present. "Eggs have three separate parts. Without all three parts, the egg would be impossible. They need each other to work, even though each part of the egg has a very different function. The three of us have very different roles. But like the egg, we need each other to be complete."

God managed to explain something complex to me in terms that I could understand. He loves to share his mysteries—with each one of us.

Mr. Postman

"Come unto me all ye that labour and are heavy laden, and I will give you rest." (Matthew 11:28)

I once heard a minister say that each set of eyes we meet are eyes that are loved by Christ. Sometimes, we learn extraordinary lessons about God's love from people who are going about the ordinary business of being themselves.

It was a smoldering July day when I entered a fast-food restaurant with my two young children. The sky above was a clear robin-egg blue without the slightest hint of a cloud anywhere. Sweltering heat rose up in visible waves, as we gratefully exchanged the blistering sun beating down on us for the coolness of an air-conditioned building.

We picked up our tray loaded with food and soft drinks, and the three of us made our way to a booth near the back of the building. Our bare, sweaty legs squeaked softly against the shiny vinyl-padded bench, as we slid comfortably into our seats. I dealt out the steaming-hot burgers and fries to my hungry children, and as I did, my eyes lifted momentarily to meet the smiling gaze of a middle-aged mailman sitting across the aisle from us. He seemed amused by the little hands grabbing for food like hungry birds eager to be fed.

It was impossible not to notice how brightly his cheeks glowed after delivering the morning mail. Large beads of sweat peppered his neatly combed, dark, thinning hair. What should have been a crisp, blue, postal-issued uniform had been transformed by the sweltering summer day into soggy, wrinkled garments that looked like they had just been removed from a washing machine and put back on before they could find their way to the dryer.

I returned the smile and went back to the task of feeding my children. I felt sympathy for this man who would shortly put himself back on the streets to finish his route.

We pulled the waxy paper off our burgers and dumped crispy fries onto our trays so they could be dipped into ketchup squeezed out of shiny little packets. As the first morsels of food hit our mouths, a young man passed by our table and slid into the booth directly in front of us.

He was easy to recognize. His pale, rather-pudgy, pear-shaped face had been a familiar sight on the front pages of our local newspaper for weeks. He had been accused of murdering a young woman friend, and for many days the sad story of her death was in the headlines of all the local media. Moment-by-moment events of his well-publicized trial were devoured by the people of Fargo, as they heard about the girl who died too young and too violently.

My friends and I discussed the case over and over again. Perhaps we thought that by talking about it, we could make some sense of the tragedy. But murder never makes sense. The crime was rare and unthinkable in the seventies, especially in our usually tranquil and quiet community.

Without hesitation, my doting and protective motherly instincts revved into high gear, and I fought the urge to gather my precious young chicks protectively under my wings and run. How ridiculous would it have been to dash out of the building with one bewildered child tucked firmly under each arm? Besides, we hardcore Scandinavians don't display our emotions for the world to see if there is any possible way to prevent it.

With little success, I tried to find a comfortable spot in the room where I could fix my gaze. Finally, I stared intently at the hamburger lodged firmly between my teeth, perched two inches below my lowered eyes. Was it my imagination, or was the mailman's smile just a little broader than it had been a moment ago? My eyes quickly darted back to the half-eaten piece of meat and away from the amused grin, obviously directed at me.

The sweaty, young man sitting an arm's length from our table, slouched lazily across the long bench. He was a large man, and his legs hung out into the aisle. The weight of his thick body rested heavily on one elbow as he brought his food slowly to his mouth with his free hand. His slightly slanted eyes hunted uncertainly around the room, perhaps monitoring the crowd's reaction to his presence.

According to the news reports, his IQ measured low, as did the IQ of his unfortunate female friend. Her remains were found floating in the dark waters of the local river that ran along the eastern border of our city. There seemed little doubt about this man's guilt, yet he was acquitted of the crime, and to my knowledge, no one else was ever sought in the case.

The pleasant expression on the mail carrier's face continued without interruption, as much to my surprise, and his obvious amusement, the postal carrier greeted the young man sitting across from him by name. With complete genuineness, and all the respect one would afford a visiting dignitary, the postman invited the young lad to join him. Calmly munching his lunch, the young man snarled a defiant *no*. Still smiling, the postman refused to be dissuaded, and after some gentle, persistent prodding, the untidy accused finally agreed to the short move, and lopped sluggishly across the aisle with his tray in hand. The mailman smiled at me with a knowing grin.

Embarrassed to be caught staring, my eyes moved away from the scene once again. With a mouth full of lunch that had long ago lost its taste, I suddenly understood how Alice must have felt as she tumbled helplessly through the looking glass. No matter how hard I tried, I simply couldn't figure out where normal was in this situation.

To put it generously, the young man was filthy. His clothes reeked with a staggering mixture of body odor and dirt, that radiated from him like a piece of limburger cheese sizzling on a hot summer stove. Vile, disgusting words tumbled carelessly out of his mouth in long, rambling succession, aimed at no one or anything in particular. Every inch of me wanted to protect my children's tender, young ears from the unexplained profanity floating heavily through the air behind them.

Thankfully, the lunch and the amusement provided on the children's placemats, seemed ample diversion from the constant stream of four-letter words spinning behind their heads. They simply seemed not to notice.

Mr. Postman's smile remained genuine and unaffected, as he kindly asked his luncheon guest why he talked like that. The mail carrier's quiet, caring resolve, disarmed the intense young fellow for a moment as he held his food in his mouth without chewing it. Silently, curiously, he searched the gentle sincerity on the mailman's face. For a moment, he seemed confused by this rare, unexplained kindness, as the mail carrier's words floated toward him in soothing tones.

I have to admit that I was more than a bit bewildered by the host's generous attitude toward his luncheon guest myself. Within a few seconds, the person with his back to me regained his momentum, and another stream of vile expletives rolled off his wide lips with renewed enthusiasm.

If the postman wasn't enjoying lunch with his companion, he took absolutely no steps to hide the sheer look of delight on his face as he monitored my futile attempt not to be astonished at the whole surreal scene unfolding before my eyes. How could the mailman eat with the overwhelming stench of foul body odor floating up from the shaggy body staring blankly at him from across the table, to say nothing of the salty language that made my mouth sag despite what I considered a valiant effort to keep my lips together? The postman seemed not to notice the negative aspects of this young person that were so obvious to me. His eyes continued to sparkle, and the ever-present kindly smile never left his face. He treated the accused as one would treat a cherished brother or a treasured friend: precious and valuable.

Slowly, and with no small amount of embarrassment, I realized that I could read about Christianity, I could talk to others about

God's love and have a friendship with Christ. But this humble mailman *lived* Christ.

Christ accepts us the way the postman accepted his luncheon companion. We come to our Savior bearing a multitude of different conditions. Sometimes we arrive with only enough energy to carry one small flicker of hope. We often come to Jesus filthy, disgusting, stinking, exhausted, depressed, out of answers, reeking with sin, desperate with hopelessness, or just needing an answer for our lives.

Christ runs to each of us with open, embracing arms, as he joyfully welcomes us into his heart—just the way we are.

Just a Dollar

"Oh taste and see that the Lord is good. Blessed is the man that trusteth in him." (Psalm 23:8)

My dad and his army buddy Cliff Horken started the H&H Company, Hendrickson and Horken, after World War II, with two rows of paint on the store shelves. My father said that they were fortunate to get that much product. Everything was scarce after the war.

In time the store grew. Carpet and linoleum were added, along with shoes. At some point it became clear that supporting two growing families would be difficult with a small business in a tiny town, so my dad bought out Cliff's ownership, and the Horkens moved on.

I have no idea what I was doing at the store that day. My guess is that my mother had a commitment for the afternoon, so I was turned over to my father's care. Dad ran the store without help, except for the Aase brothers who painted and laid flooring for him. Entertaining a four-year-old for five hours was no easy task. Dad gave me a paintbrush and put me to work dusting the tops of the paint cans. After a while, the job became boring, so I began to search for something else to do.

I skipped over to Joe Soderberg's Appliance Store. His business adjoined my father's, and it was a magical place. Shiny new refrigerators and stoves rested neatly against the walls. Washers and dryers sat in the middle of his store. All of Joe's appliances were pink, while our appliances at home were everyday white. Joe let me pretend that the dazzling appliances were mine, and I played house in his store for a long time. After a while, the fun became old, and Joe's hospitality was running a little thin, so I popped back to Dad's store to see what entertainment I could find there.

A man came into the store, so Dad sat me at his desk while he attended to the customer's needs. *Wow! My very own typewriter and adding machine.* Before long, all the keys on the typewriter had jammed together, so I yelled for my dad to come and help me.

"Mary, I'm busy with a customer. You'll just have to wait."

Not one of my favorite words. I sat in a heap at my father's desk, waiting. And that is when I saw it: a dollar bill, lying under the glass that covered the surface of my father's desk.

With the customer gone and my eyes bright with hope, I said, "Dad. Can I have that dollar?" I mean, do the arithmetic. My allowance was five cents a week, and a dollar was about five months' pay. Really? How many men can say no to their little girl? But that is exactly what my father said to me.

"That dollar doesn't belong to me," my dad explained patiently.

"Who does it belong to?" I wanted to know.

"A man came in here one day and bought something and overpaid me—with this dollar. And if he ever comes back to the store again, I will give it to him."

"How will you know him?"

"I remember what he looks like."

My heart sank. All hope was gone. The dollar was not to be mine.

The H&H Company closed its doors in 1991, a year after my father passed away. As we cleared off his desk, we found his Bible that had been sitting there since he had opened the store in 1945. Inside the cover was written, "The H&H Company in partnership with God." And under the glass on dad's desk sat the dollar bill where my father had placed it forty-six years before, still waiting for the return of its owner.

Honestly God

"Let us therefore come boldly before the throne of grace." (Hebrews 4:16)

Anyone who raises children will tell you that the bathroom can be a safe haven, a sanctuary where you can grab a few moments of much-needed solitude. Occasionally, the bolted door, with the parent on one side and the child on the other side, can save the child's life and the parent from a lengthy stay in a six-by-six cage.

Many years ago, when my children were still toddlers, a friend of mine lost her baby. He was born with a serious heart defect. Yet all indications were that with the proper medical care, the baby would grow up and live a normal life. Then suddenly, he was gone.

I had prayed. And I had believed that the baby would be well. Now I was angry and confused. I felt that God had betrayed the faith that I had placed in him. Everything came to a head one afternoon as I was perched on the bathroom stool.

What an embarrassing place to be struck by lightning, I thought to myself. But I couldn't keep the hurt and anger over the loss of my friend's child pent up any longer.

"I *HATE* you," I exploded at God. "How could you let this baby die? I know you could have made him better."

No lightning. Just the sound of God laughing.

"Good. You've finally been honest with me," he said. "Now you can say anything to me without ever having to worry about it again."

Feeling that what I had said, and the manner with which it was said, showed a total lack of respect to God. Yet through that experience, I learned that being honest with God is not being disrespectful at all. He deserved to hear what was in my heart, because he knew how I was feeling long before the words erupted all over this most private of rooms.

We owe it to God to come clean with our feelings. Nothing hidden in our hearts can be dealt with if we don't take the time to sit face-to-face with our Father and share with him our hurts and our frustrations. Even our disappointments and our anger.

Walking on Water

"And it shall come to pass in the last days, saith God, I will pour out my Spirit upon all flesh: and your sons and your daughters shall prophesy, and your young men shall see visions, and your old men shall dream dreams."
(Acts 2:17)

There is a secret way by which we can touch the very heart of God. It is in the intimate place of praising him that he blesses us for setting aside our own wants and concerns. Praising allows him to become the center of our attention.

Anyone who has had a near-death experience and has returned to tell about it, or has seen a brilliant angel, will often tell you that there are no adequate words to describe what they have seen. That is what happened to me one evening.

While spending time sitting before God and praising him, I suddenly found myself transported from our family room to a virtually unfamiliar land. Believe me when I say that this place looked nothing like the vast and open plains of North Dakota.

I was seated very high on a rocky cliff overlooking a golden, motionless sea. The air was still and warm. Sitting upon the tranquil body of water below me was a large sailing vessel with several looming masts, and on the deck of the boat was a handsomely rugged, muscular, olive-skinned man busily mending the ship's sails. A light tan bandana was wound securely around his forehead to keep the sweat from dripping down his face. Rings of dark curls fell slightly over the piece of cloth. Even though it seemed as if I were a long distance away from the stranger on the boat, I could clearly see the beads of sweat on his muscular body.

At some point, he turned around and slowly lifted his eyes upward, gazing at the jagged rocks where I sat. He seemed as surprised to see me as I was to be there, yet there was no acknowledgment of my presence. Instead, he quietly returned to his work.

A soft haze fell across the beautifully painted sky, reflecting pools of golden hues upon the still waters. Whatever land I had accidentally stumbled into, it was one of perfect tranquility and peace. Time didn't seem to exist in this place.

Feeling perfectly content, I lingered comfortably, perched on the beautiful rocks high above the waves that gently lapped upon the sand. Sometime in the soft, golden glow of this glorious place, it dawned on me that the man working beneath my vantage point was Christ, stealing a rare moment where he could be alone. Something about his demeanor imparted to me that his work on the ship was not a job at all but a way of relaxation for him.

While gazing down at him, it was easy to see that this was a place he loved, and working on the boat brought contentment. I was an intruder. Yet it was such a personal and intimate look at Jesus that I could not will myself to leave or to remove my eyes from him.

When his work was finished and the sails were returned to their proper place, the man on the boat quietly invited me to join him, and we both climbed effortlessly into the ship. We knew each other's thoughts, yet I don't remember any exchange of words. In fact, words would have only served to diminish the experience as we glided slowly upon the golden waters.

I remember so well the soft, quiet ripples as the vessel sailed effortlessly over them. We basked in the warmth of the love and peace permeating that time and place. To this day, when I need to be alone with Jesus, in my heart, I climb back into that boat, leaving everything behind, taking with me the thanks, joys, and concerns I want to share with Christ.

It had been several years since I shared this intimate time with Christ, but we had a week of tragedy that made us want to hide our telephone. News that a friend's son had been killed in a terrible car accident, along with five other people, reached us on what had started out to be a quiet Saturday night. The next morning during our church service, we learned of the tragic death of one of our church member's daughters: another car accident. Her death hitting way too close to home, this lovely young woman was a year younger than our daughter.

For months, the husband of a friend of ours was told that his illness was simply a lingering case of the flu. By the time his *three-month flu* was correctly diagnosed as cancer, there was nothing anyone could do to save his life. One of our daughter's coworkers found out that his beautiful three-year-old daughter had a rare form of cancer that brought her young life to an end with terrifying speed.

Calling upon Christ, we climbed into the ship and sailed upon the now-familiar, comfortable waters. I needed to get away with him; away from all the pain that my friends were experiencing, away from the solemn knowledge that I had no power to ease their suffering.

"Would you like to walk on the water?" Christ asked in a gentle tone.

I was surprised, and thinking that death would be the only vehicle by which this could possibly happen, I politely but firmly declined.

Christ smiled and said, "Don't be afraid. I'll hold your hand."

So out of the boat we went.

I gazed down through the crystal clear water. Fish swam calmly beneath our feet, easily maneuvering their way through magnificently colored pastel coral reefs.

For me, the experience of walking on water was not a comfortable one. Nothing was definite. There were no paths to follow, no sense of being in control of anything. Walking on water was like walking on Jell-O. There was nothing solid beneath us, and I desperately wanted to get back into the boat with its firmness and protection.

Searching anxiously across the water for the sailing vessel, I suddenly realized that it was nowhere in sight. All that was left was a never-ending sea—and Christ holding my hand, reassuring me that there was nothing left for me but to trust him.

For all the people mentioned above, and countless others, their boat is gone too. Their life has suddenly taken a turn into sad and unfamiliar territory, and the secure vessel that had been their life would never return to them the same. They are left to walk on water, but they do not have to walk alone. No matter how difficult the circumstances, Christ promises to hold us up above the waves when we are too weak or injured to carry on alone.

Precious

*"Commit thy way unto the Lord; trust also in him,
and he shall bring it to pass." (Psalm 37:5)*

Back in the sixties, a friend of mine was a student of nursing at the Hennepin County General Hospital in Minneapolis. As Betty's class became more proficient in their studies, they began rotating shifts on the wards, not just during the day, but also at night.

One evening, a friend of Betty's was assigned to the NICU, a nursery where premature or very ill babies are cared for. At that time, technology was in its infancy, and medications to help tiny babies survive were very few.

As Betty's friend was caring for one of the babies in the unit, she looked up and noticed that the medical resident on duty that night had draped himself over one of the incubators holding an infant who was very critically ill. Interns and residents worked insanely long hours, and Betty's friend assumed that the doctor was taking a moment to rest.

She walked over to him and gently placed her hand on his shoulder. "Why don't you go upstairs and get some rest?" she suggested quietly to the doctor. "The baby seems to be all right for now. I'll call you if there is any change."

The young doctor lifted his head and stood up. With a smile on his face, he said, "Nurse, I'm not tired. It's just that I have done everything that I can for this child. There's nothing more that I can think of that I can do to help her. I was just placing her into God's hands."

Sometimes, someone whom we have never seen, never met, travels into our heart without ever knowing it, leaving gentle little footprints behind them.

A Tap at the Window

"Ah Lord God! Behold, thou has made the heaven and the earth by thy great power and stretched out arm, and there is nothing too hard for thee." (Jeremiah 32:7)

I have always believed that our best traits are often our worst, and mine is a mutant rescue gene. Forget about my children bringing stray animals home. It was always me. Every homeless critter was taken in, loved, and cared for.

In the late 1970s, we purchased a vacant home in a quiet Fargo neighborhood. Shortly before our move-in date, we decided to tour the yard to see if we could get a head start on anything that needed our attention. The subdivision was very new, and there were no trees or fences for as far as we could see, except for one tiny, pathetic, eight-foot twig lying horizontally on the south side of our soon-to-be house.

The previous owners had placed the hose from the sump pump next to the tree before they moved, hoping I suppose, that the water would keep the tree alive. In fact, their good intentions accomplished just the opposite. The soil around the *almost* tree was so saturated that the little branch was drowning, and the ground had softened to the point where the wispy twig had simply tumbled over. What little root system the tree possessed, pointed directly skyward.

True to my nature, I suggested to my husband that the tree deserved a chance to live. He rightfully pronounced the tree *dead*.

It certainly didn't take a genius to see what was obvious to him. Yet I couldn't stand the thought of pulling the few remaining roots out of the ground and discarding the little sprig, so I pleaded my case one more time.

My husband gave me one of his long defeated, "I may as well get to this task because there is no winning here" looks, and headed for the garden to retrieve some drier soil. Our soon-to-be next-door neighbor appeared and offered us the use of his wheelbarrow and a shovel. No doubt he went home and suggested to his wife that the lady moving into the house next door was clinically delusional.

Together, Dick and I packed fresh black dirt around our well-meaning but questionable project, until the roots were neatly tucked back into place. Then my husband, who didn't even attempt to feign an ounce of enthusiasm, tied rope around the beanstalk of a branch and staked it firmly to the ground. When the chore was finished, it appeared that we had just positioned a dead tree upright in our yard. It looked seriously ridiculous.

Our North Dakota winters are usually brutal. But not that winter. The temperatures hovered in the fifties and sixties, which seemed to give my noble mission a fighting chance. By spring, our little *rescue twig* was showing signs of life. Subtle signs mind you, but nevertheless, there was a glimmer of hope growing outside of my kitchen window.

Another year passed. While there were no monumental advances in the *ridiculous rescue* department, my husband murmured something about the possibility of the tree surviving. After another year went by, we were able to remove the stakes that had anchored the fragile branch. And even though the crown of our twig had a rather odd list toward the east, it stood on its own. It was a proud moment.

That Christmas, my son and husband covered the branches of my tree with twinkling white lights. We pronounced our tree *adorable*. However, within three years, the lights that had given us so much Christmas joy were dangling from their electrical cords, snapped apart as the tree spread upward and outward. Our little twig was becoming a giant.

In a few more years, the tree was the tallest in the neighborhood, and the messiest. It wasn't quite so adorable anymore. We discovered from someone who actually knew a thing or two about trees, that the tree living outside of our kitchen window was a cottonwood. The man who had previously owned our house was an agronomist. Whatever was he thinking when he planted that thing? Cottonwoods are arguably one of the messiest trees in the world. At least I could plead ignorance.

Every spring, long, sticky, lacy seed casings fell from the tree, everywhere. They landed in our rock gardens and had to be blown out with a leaf blower. They fell all over our yard and all over our neighbors' yards. And in the fall, the leaves, thousands of them, repeated the process. Not only that, but months after the last respectable leaf had blown off every other tree in our yard, and our neighbors' yards, my tree was still hanging on to its offspring.

Come spring, not only did we have the seed casings to deal with, but we still had a whole yard full of soggy, leftover leaves from the previous fall. I came to despise that tree. With more than a hint of sarcastic victory, my husband would gently but knowingly ask, "Remember who wanted to save that tree?" There was no choice but to cease complaining, at least outwardly.

In the late 1990s, our part of the country suffered through some very long and difficult winters. We were hit with one blizzard after another, along with relentless days of below-zero temperatures. It was on one particularly cold, cold day that my little *rescue tree* found a way to show its gratitude to me for saving its life.

Even in North Dakota we have dishwashers. But for some reason, I was standing at the kitchen sink washing dishes, when I heard the tapping of a branch against the window above me. My tree. I glanced up and murmured, *Oh be quiet.* (I know. Talking to a tree, right?) Again, the branch tapped against the bay window, to which I impatiently growled, "I *hate* you. You are nothing but a nuisance. Leave me alone." My eyes sank down to the soapy water once again.

Still, the persistent branch continued knocking until finally in frustration, I looked up. My mouth dropped as I saw something that I had never noticed before. My tree was pregnant.

On that day, the sky was a deep, icy, slate blue, the temperature, a nasty minus-twenty-two degrees. Mounds of deep, bleak snow covered the terrain. Yet my little tree was gleefully—and persistently, I might add—shouting, "Look at me! I am exploding with life!" And so it was. Thousands of dainty, delicate, pink buds were curiously poking their heads out of hugely swollen pods, swaying with joyful abandon in the breeze.

I stood at the window for a very long time, bathing in the miracle before me. Through my little tree, God showed me that he is the author of life, and the starkness of death that winter brings, has no power to destroy it.

The Lord Is My Shepherd

"I am the good shepherd: the good shepherd giveth his life for the sheep." (John 10:11)

Rain in the Red River Valley never falls straight out of the heavens. Valleys are windy, and our weather is almost always accompanied to the tune of some sort of breeze. At times, the wind is gentle. More often than not, it is a "Hang on, Toto" kind of day.

On a gloomy Sunday afternoon, my husband Dick was snuggled under a quilt, catching up on much-needed rest from his busy workweek. The children were playing at the homes of friends. And outside, it was pouring. Perhaps the rain was especially memorable because it resembled the scene from the gazebo in the movie *The Sound of Music*. There was no wind. Instead of the predictable slant, the water fell to the saturated earth in straight lines.

Quietly, I slid into the driver's seat of my car and backed out of the garage. My spirits, matching the weather, needed a little lifting. "Where are you, God?" I whispered quietly. The only reply was the sound of raindrops hitting my windshield.

As I headed south on Elm Street, I asked God what he wanted to talk about. Why does it always amaze me when he is so eager to answer that question? His reply was immediate: "I want to talk about the Twenty-Third Psalm."

"No! No, no, no. Do you see how dreary it is out here?" I inquired of God, as if he was oblivious to the current weather conditions.

He laughed a little, then said, "You're wrong. The Twenty-Third Psalm isn't depressing at all. Let me tell you how I meant the psalm to be understood."

So I listened, and he shared his wisdom about this magnificent passage.

The Lord is my Shepherd: "But you don't always want me. Often, you would rather go your own way." *I shall not want.*

He maketh me to lie down in green pastures: "I force you to lie down, because sometimes you need to rest. I don't lead you to muddy, empty pastures. I take you to pastures that are lush and green: that are full of all good things, because I love you."

He leadeth me beside still waters: "I lead you not beside waters that are angry, full of tension, and danger. I lead you to a place of peace."

He restoreth my soul: "Because you have no power to do it on your own."

He leadeth me in the paths of righteousness for his name's sake: "Because it brings honor to me."

Yea though I walk through the valley of the shadow of death, I will fear no evil: for thou art with me: "When your life is in danger, as the Good Shepherd, I place myself between you and that danger. With the weapons available to me as your Shepherd, I will protect you." *Thy rod and thy staff, they comfort me."*

Thou preparest a table before me: "Not only do I bless you, I do it in front of those who hate you and want to harm or destroy you." *In the presence of mine enemies.*

Thou anointest my head with oil. "Oil is the symbol for the Holy Spirit. I don't just dab a little on your forehead. I dump it all over you in generous amounts."

My cup runneth over: "My blessings are so abundant that you cannot begin to contain them."

MARY EMERSON

Surely—goodness—and mercy—shall follow me—all the days of my life: "And when that life is over, you will live where I live—forever and forever." *And I will dwell in the house of the Lord forever.*

God's lesson had ended. Despite the continual flow of rain and dreary, gray clouds covering the sky, my heart was warmed by the sunshine of his words.

Listen Quietly

"Fear thou not, for I am with thee. Be not dismayed, for I am thy God; I will strengthen thee; yea, I will help thee."
(Isaiah 41:10)

The odor of spices from freshly baked molasses cookies filled the air. One-by-one, I slid the cookies off the baking sheets and onto cooling racks. The house smelled like Christmas. My eyes moved from the kitchen to the crèche sitting in our living room.

Who were you? I wondered as I looked at the statue of Mary. *What was it about you that so endeared you to God that he chose you to have his baby, to be his mother? For that matter, to be his wife?*

What a rotten place for a king, a savior to be born—for anyone to be born, I thought, as I returned to my Christmas baking.

The serene crèche gave no hint about what Mary must have gone through to reach that stable. Imagine the look on her parents' faces when they found out that their child was pregnant out of wedlock, and the father was God. Try to explain that to your mom and dad. Her friends may have abandoned her.

And until an angel paid a visit to Joseph to explain Mary's pregnancy to him, he abandoned her as well.

I asked Mary how she managed to handle what must have been a fearful and lonely time in her life. Would she really answer me?

Tenderly, the Mary whom I knew so little about, the Mary whom I had completely dismissed from my life and my faith, sat across from me, and with gentle grace, she answered me.

"I trusted God," she said softly. "No matter what happened, I trusted God. I trusted him to take care of us. I never stopped trusting God."

I now know a little more about the woman whom God chose to carry his child: the woman who was to become God's mother. She taught me the importance of trusting God no matter how difficult the circumstances in life might be.

Don't be afraid to ask what you are curious about. You might be amazed at what you hear.

He's Back

"He that believeth in me hath everlasting life." (John 6:47)

There is only one person whom I can think of whose birth announcement was made by a sky full of magnificent angels singing about a baby who was born in a barn and lying in a food trough for animals. With unspeakable joy and pride, the angels declared his arrival to a group of rugged, unkempt shepherds, as they watched for the safety of their sheep on the hills near the little village of Bethlehem. No person in this world could ever claim that they were too poor to approach the Christ child, for he was born in the lowliest of places. He would be a shepherd, too. And like any good shepherd, his job would be to care for and protect his flock.

There is another day in the life of Christ: a day that will change the world forever. Caroling angels are replaced by the haunting cadence of drums as a heavy wooden cross thumps softly along a dusty road on its path to the Skull of the Rock. A frenzied mob of onlookers jeer wildly as they follow the convicted criminal struggling with the burden of the tree he carries on his shoulders. Abandoned by his friends and his followers, he will make the trip to the cross alone. It is a chosen path. He will die in your place—and in mine.

On the night before Christ's death, Jesus and his disciples celebrate the Jewish Feast of the Passover in a room nestled somewhere within the city of Jerusalem. This will be the last time he will dine with his friends before his death. Humbly, his heart full of love and gratitude to his loyal disciples who gave up everything in their lives to follow him, he kneels before each one, tenderly washing their feet. It is his final gift to them before his death.

There must have been tremendous sadness in his heart as he came to Judas. No one can hurt us like a friend who deceives us. Of course, Judas was not the only the person to betray Christ that night. Before morning, his dearest friend, the disciple Peter, insisted passionately to three different people that he had never met Jesus.

When the evening meal was finished, the little band of Christians moved unnoticed to the peaceful Garden of Gethsemane. If there was ever a time when Jesus needed his companions, it was now. Three times he pleaded with them to pray for him as he moved farther into the garden to be alone with his Father. Three times they meant well but lapsed into sleep. Perhaps they were tired—or just bored. Christ returned to them a fourth time and softly whispered, "Sleep on. You will need your rest tonight."

At first, the noise was just a slight din in the background as the Roman soldiers hit the ground in parade fashion unison. But before long, the sound of marching feet pounded in deafening steps of authority as they descended upon the serene garden that quietly surrounded Jesus and his little band of followers. Certainly Christ must have heard the troops advance in his direction. Certainly he had time to find a hiding place. But he was here to make a payment. The price was his life in exchange for ours. And so, he waited. As Jesus bravely faced the soldiers, asking them, "Whom do ye seek?" Judas quickly identified him as the criminal they were searching for by the betraying kiss he planted softly on the Master's cheek. Christ was arrested.

The whip used by the soldiers to beat Jesus contained steel-like pieces of bone. Each lash embedded the jagged edges into his back, ripping his flesh the length of the stripe. Flogging was meant to bring the prisoner to the point of death, not to kill him. The Roman guards viciously mocked him as they flung a robe over his torn and battered body, and when the blood from his gapping wounds clotted, the garment was jerked off his shredded back, ripping the sores open once again. Crowning his head with a cap of thick thorns, the soldiers spit at him as they watched streams of blood run down his beaten and bruised face. By now, Jesus was unrecognizable.

Weakened from the ferocious floggings, globs of spit hanging from him, he was marched ceremoniously from one powerful official to another all night long. Despised and hated by those who were jealous of him, the Pharisees and priests searched for someone in authority to seal their desire to kill him. Certainly the pious officials of the synagogues who cried—in fact, demanded—his death, didn't want Christ's blood on their hands. No one did. Eventually, he was turned over to the clambering hordes of people who chanted enthusiastically, "Crucify him! Crucify him!" And so the matter was decided.

Exhausted from lack of sleep, Jesus was dragged for hours from one end of the city to the other as the soldiers searched for someone in authority willing to condemn him. After being sentenced by Pilate, he was forced to carry the instrument of his execution to Golgotha, helped only when he buckled under the weight of the massive tree. Once there, he was compelled to lie upon the heavy wooden cross where huge, long spikes were driven into his wrists and his ankles. With nails as the only anchor supporting his body, he was hoisted up upon a hill for everyone to see.

Crucifixion is a cruel death. The condemned pushes himself up with his legs in order to get oxygen into his lungs, as he slowly and painfully suffocates.

"If you are the Messiah, why don't you save yourself?" the crowds taunted haughtily as they pointed an accusing finger at him.

How could they understand? He hadn't come to save himself. He had come to save them. All he had to do was say one word and ten thousand angels would rescue him in an instant. But for our sakes, he chose to stay. God must have wanted more than anything to snatch his son from the cross. To hold him and comfort him. To caress his wounded body and his injured soul. What a lonely day that must have been for God. His suffering must have been unspeakable.

Sometime around noon, the sky turned midnight black, and an angry wind blew across the steep, jagged rocks of Golgotha. The earth began to quake, and the time to observe the Sabbath was near. It was decided that the executions needed to be accelerated. So the soldiers broke the legs of the two criminals hanging on either side of Jesus. No longer able to push their bodies up for the air needed to fill their lungs, death came rapidly for these men.

But as the soldiers turned to break the legs of Jesus, they were amazed to find that he was already dead. Christ knew when his suffering was enough, when the payment for our souls was complete. His departure from this earth was by his own power and at the time of his own choosing.

Satan had won. He was ruler now. God was dead.

Or was he?

Christ promised he would return from the grave three days after his death, but who would believe such a ridiculous claim? The Roman soldiers guarding his tomb didn't believe it; nevertheless, they watched over the sepulcher just to make sure. The Jewish people didn't believe it. His disciples, who had witnessed astonishing miracles at his hands, didn't believe it. The three women who dutifully awoke early on Easter Sunday morning to prepare his body for burial, didn't believe it either. Not one person believed for a moment that Christ would fulfill his promise to conquer death and return to earth alive in three days.

We have the choice to believe what we want to, but unbelief does not have the power to prevent God from keeping his promises. God still did what he said he would do, despite the fact that no one believed that the resurrection would take place. Three days after the crucifixion of his Son, Jesus returned from the dead to deliver to us his gift of eternal life. He bought our souls from the devil by trading his own life for us at Calvary.

Who Is Your Favorite Person in the Bible?

"He went to Pilate and begged the body of Jesus." (Matthew 27:58)

Traveling wasn't easy that day. Dense fog floated eerily in front of me, making it difficult to see. Fog is so quiet, and so was God's voice asking me, "Who is your favorite person in the Bible?"

"Well," I answered as I peeked around the wispy clouds tiptoeing across my windshield. "There are so many amazing people in the Bible who deserve to be anyone's favorite." God and Jesus, of course. Still, besides them, I knew. I knew right away who that person was.

"Joseph. Joseph of Arimathea," I quickly replied.

No one wanted to be associated with Jesus on the day that he was crucified. The Roman soldiers were masters of excruciatingly cruel executions. His once-loyal friends distanced themselves as far from him as they possibly could. His best friend Peter denied ever knowing him, three times.

Where were those who had received his gift of healing? Where were the followers who were amazed by his wisdom and touched by his love? No one wanted to share Christ's fate, and who could blame them? Still, there was one man. One man who was willing to die so that Christ's remains would be respected after his death.

Joseph must have known how dangerous his request would be. Yet he went to Pilate and pleaded for the body of his friend. Perhaps

Pilate was relieved to have this man *Jesus* out of his life forever. There are accounts that Pilate washed his hands repeatedly for the rest of his life as he tried to remove Christ's blood and the role he played in his death.

With Pilate's blessing, Joseph pulled the spikes out of Christ's hands and feet, and lovingly lifted him down from the cross. Protecting his precious cargo, he transported the unrecognizable body of his Savior and placed it into the sepulcher that Joseph had prepared for his own death.

As God's heart shattered for his son and Christ's heart shattered for us on that somber Friday, I will forever love Joseph for risking his own life in order to honor the Lord he adored, when almost everyone else abandoned him at the time of his death.

Whiskers

"Praise the Lord of hosts: for the Lord is good." (Jeremiah 33:1)

Even though I could only see the bottom of his garment, I knew that the man standing in front of me was God. There was a spirit of awe and reverence in the room. Every color of the rainbow was richly woven into every thread of his magnificent, shimmering robe. The beauty and texture took my breath away. Slowly, my eyes inched upward until they reached God's face.

His eyes were focused straight ahead. He seemed not to notice me, acting as if I was not there at all. In fact, he hardly seemed to be there either. My mouth dropped in shock at what I saw. Whiskers! Whiskers everywhere. Whiskers growing wildly in every possible direction.

Stunned, my heart thumping, I turned my face away from his and anxiously fled from his presence.

The next day, as I read my devotions, I shielded my eyes with my hand to avert any contact with God. Still reeling from the unexpected, certainly undignified sight that I had experienced the night before, the last thing I wanted to see was God's face. Not today.

God didn't seem very anxious to leave me alone. Determined to finish the work he had begun, God asked me if I ever wondered why he had given men *whiskers*.

"No!" I replied, staring intently at the page I was reading. Quite frankly, I didn't care, nor did I want to know the answer to his question.

Seeming oblivious to my discomfort, God carried on, determined to make his point. "I gave men whiskers because I want every man to remember that when he looks in the mirror every day of his life, he is no longer a child. He is an adult. He is responsible to himself, his work, his family. He is responsible to me."

I lifted my eyes to my Father's smiling face. His whiskers were neatly back in place.

"Thank you, Father. Thank you. For sharing your wisdom—and your delicious sense of humor."

Who Touched Me?

"If I may but touch his garment, I shall be whole." (Matthew 9:21)

There were very few times in my adult life when I wanted my mother to take care of me. But when I was sick, running a fever, my head exploding from all that icky nose stuff that comes from *God only knows where*, I wanted my mother. I wanted her to smile at me and pretend that she was not concerned as she tucked a cozy, warm quilt around my neck—the way she did when I was a little child.

I wanted her to bring a bowl of streaming hot soup on a tray to my bedside, with little saltine crackers to crumble into the warm liquid. I wanted my mother to bring Kleenex to wipe my uncontrollable drippy nose, and a cup of hot chocolate full of tiny white miniature marshmallows swimming in circles on the top. Not that it would make me feel better, but she did it because she knew that I loved hot chocolate, and she wanted me to find something I could be happy about, if just for a few minutes.

I wanted to wake up in the middle of the night and see my mother's face staring down at mine with concern. It was the one time in my life when I wanted her to be the caregiver while I just laid back and became a child again.

There was a woman who lived during the time that Christ was on the earth. She had been sick for twelve years, and the doctors had no cure for her. She must have been excruciatingly lonely. She was an outcast because of the laws in place at that time to protect the community from illness. Those who were sick were considered unclean. Someone to be shunned, avoided.

It is amazing how word spread from village to village about Christ's ministry and his travels at a time when there were no television sets, radios, telephones, or computers to post his schedule. Yet inevitably, wherever Christ appeared, crowds of people knew about his coming, and they eagerly awaited his arrival.

We really don't know how this woman heard about Christ's upcoming visit or of his reputation as a healer. People said that this man by his gentle touch could heal the blind, the deaf, and those who were ill. Would she dare to hope that Jesus would have the answer for her? Who was she to ask for such a favor? Would Christ ignore her pleas and pull away from a woman whom no one wanted to touch? Would she have to live one more time with crushing disappointment? Still, she was determined to try.

On the day of Christ's arrival, the woman blended in with the crowd of people as they hurried down the dusty village path to seek the young *Miracle Worker*. But by the time that she made her way toward Jesus, he was already surrounded by eager onlookers, desiring a touch from him for their needs too. Reaching him must have seemed impossible. Perhaps the expectation of finding help hidden so tenderly in her heart turned from hope to despair.

Most of the people were strong. She was not. She cried out to the physician, but her voice dissolved among the sound of so many other voices. Christ would be gone in a second. If she could not reach him now, right now, her miracle would be lost forever.

At the risk of being trampled to death, the woman boldly stretched out her arms and threw herself toward the back of Christ's feet, landing with a thud in the middle of the road. What a pitiful sight she must have been, lying on her stomach, motionless in the dirt. Perhaps her arms were scraped and bloodied, her clothing soiled and torn, her face full of dirt. Had the people in their frenzy to reach Christ trampled over her?

We do not know the details of that moment, but we do know one thing. Ever so barely, with the tip of her finger, she managed to touch the hem of Christ's garment. And in that moment, she knew it had been enough.

Immediately, Christ stopped walking. Turning to his disciples, he asked a question that must have seemed utterly ridiculous given the number of people surrounding him. "Who touched me?"

His friends must have looked at each other rather quizzically and said something like, "Are you kidding me?"

"This touch was different from the others," Christ insisted. His eyes scanned the group of men, women, and children until they fell upon the woman lying on the path beneath him, gazing up at his face.

"Why did you touch me?" Christ inquired with tender compassion.

I would have to believe that the muscular arms of the carpenter from Nazareth bent down and lifted the woman tenderly off the ground as he cradled her with his love. With dirt-streaked tears flowing softly down her pale, sunken cheeks, she expressed to Christ her utter and profound belief that he would not only understand her suffering; but in her heart, she knew that if she could only touch him, he would make her well. And so he did.

There are no ordinary people in Christ's eyes. We are not just another person lost in a never-ending sea of other people. When our lives seem hopeless, empty, lonely; when we are in pain or just desire a compassionate friend, we need only to touch the hem of his garment with our heart to get his attention.

The wonderful truth of this story is that like the woman desperate to reach her Savior, amazing things happen to us when we take a moment to touch him.

And a Little Child Shall Lead Them

"He is gracious and full of compassion." (Psalm 112:4)

Because our family lives several hours away from each other, we don't often have the opportunity to share meals together. But one Friday evening, we gathered for dinner at a popular restaurant in Minneapolis. When we were finished eating, napkins off our laps and the time for good-byes to be said, my son brought up his concern about my eyesight. No doubt he was chosen by the family to approach this subject with me, because he and I have always had a close relationship.

"You need to wear your glasses when you drive, Mom," Ryan stated in a matter-of-fact manner.

Every head at the table bobbed in agreement, meaning that the subject had been discussed behind my back before anyone had arrived at the restaurant. Even though their concern was well placed, I felt like I had just been the victim of a well-planned lynching.

Sometimes, people can be totally right and totally wrong at the same time. There was no doubt that my family meant well, but their good intentions left me feeling like I had just been kicked in the chest by a spooked horse who had just successfully knocked the wind out of me. Everyone left the restaurant in complete and uncomfortable silence. I was embarrassed and crushed.

The next morning, still licking my wounds from the previous night, I drove from our hotel to my daughter's house. Our granddaughter Erica, who is the most reliable child, had left her schoolwork undone. With a coveted ticket to the Hannah Montana concert that evening, she was in danger of missing the production in favor of catching up on her studies.

Tears ran down her tiny cheeks; her shoulders heaved as she tried to control huge sobs that escaped from her lips in sputtering little jerks. It was one of those moments that I knew my opinion was neither invited nor wanted. So I kept quiet, even though I wanted to scream "Mercy" at the top of my lungs.

When her mother finally delivered the last word of her lecture, she gathered her daughter in her arms and said, "We have to go to the store. When we get home, I'll help you with your schoolwork. We'll get it done before the concert."

Erica managed a little smile.

"Mom, do you want to drive, or do you want me to drive?" Lisa asked as she slid her arm into her coat sleeve.

Wrong question. I tossed my keys onto the counter and said, "You drive."

"Why are you mad at me? I didn't say anything."

Maybe not, but I strongly suspected that even though Lisa wasn't on the front lines, she was cheering from the bleachers. As we left the house for the car, it was my turn to dissolve into tears.

There was a pregnant silence as we drove the five miles to the mall. Lisa parked the car and walked angrily toward the door. Our grandson Zane was keeping up with her. Like a droopy dog who had just been kicked in the ribs, I lagged half a block behind everyone else. And Erica? Erica found herself hopelessly caught between two people whom she dearly loved.

First, she glanced at her mother, then gazed sympathetically in my direction. She simply didn't know what to do. Hesitating for just a moment, she turned around and walked back to me as I sauntered along with my hands thrust deeply into my coat pockets, my head pointed directly at the ground. With a compassionate and caring expression on her face, Erica tenderly slid her tiny little nine-year-old hand softly into my pocket and searched with her fingers until she found mine. She didn't say a word. She simply stared straight ahead and gently led me to the mall door.

As we reached the entrance, Erica turned and looked at me as she spoke for the first time. "We haven't had a very good day, have we, Grandma?"

It took a child to understand my pain, and I was grateful.

After a short time, I put my injured feelings behind me and explained to my daughter that I had felt outnumbered the night before. It wasn't that they were wrong. Their words had caught me off guard.

Erica's sweet spirit taught me that sometimes words aren't necessary. Her gentle, comforting touch was just the right medicine for that moment, and for my injured heart.

Expectations

"My soul, wait thou only upon God; for my expectation is from him." (Psalm 62:5)

It seems silly to go into a closet when we want to talk to God. Still, that is exactly what God invites us to do. A closet has no noise or distractions. There are no television sets or cell phones. God just wants us in a place where we can give our full attention to him, to each other.

My car is my closet. In the quietness of this small, rolling space, I can be alone with God. This is where I pray, where I pour my heart out to my Father.

Right before Christmas, I found myself alone in my car for a three-hour trip. Between a recent cataract surgery (my son was right after all) and tasks that I felt were necessary to make the holiday special for those I love, my relationship with God had been placed on the back burner—again.

Finally, I was alone. Alone with God. It's not that I wanted anything special or needed anything from him. I just wanted him.

I started thinking about the word *expectation*. *What a great word for the season*, I thought to myself. It seems as though the expectations that we place on ourselves far exceed the expectations that anyone else places on us this time of year. I started wondering what expectations God had of me. Just as important, what expectations did I have of God?

The Bible is so full of God's promises. Yet without the expectation and the faith that God meant those promises for us, nothing much happens. When our eyes are removed from our circumstances and are placed on God and his promises, amazing things happen. He is still the God of miracles, the God of his promises.

When time finally allowed me to be able to catch up to my December 24th devotions, one of the first words on the page was *expectation*. This season is so full of this word.

The anticipation of Christmas. The celebration of Christ's birth. God's gift of eternal life.

A Friend Loveth at All Times

"A friend loveth at all times." (Proverbs 17:1)

If there was ever a dream come true, it happened for me on a beautiful summer day several years ago, when I found a quaint cottage that stole my heart. The serene little house was located on an island, with just a thread of a roadway connecting it to the mainland.

Nestled amid hundreds of towering maple trees, the hexagon-shaped cabin was perched comfortably on top of a luscious grassy hill that sloped gently down to a sandy beach. Three sides of the house were glass, allowing for a panoramic view overlooking the water. The front of the house was encircled by a cedar deck, and a cozy stone fireplace separated the kitchen from the living room. My husband fell in love with the house too, and soon it became our second home.

Shortly after moving in to our little cabin, we met our next-door neighbors, Susan and Paul Christopher. Paul was the pastor of a Lutheran Church in a tiny southern Minnesota community. Sue taught kindergarten. They had three boys who were close in age to our children. Immediately, Sue and I became friends.

The first weekend after meeting the Christophers, I drove on to our property, my car bursting with children, a dog, and a couple of cats. Upon arriving, I was amazed to discover that Sue had created a path between our houses. Believe me when I say that clearing out hundreds of rambling, gnarled sticks and rugged, overgrown brush that had cluttered the property between our houses for decades, was no easy task. Our friendship was important enough to Sue to make it easier for us to get together, and I was profoundly touched by her thoughtful act of kindness.

Sue and I were so different. She had a passion for outdoor projects, always digging up the dirt in her yard to add yet "another" flower garden. From my window, I would often catch a glimpse of her mowing their yard or raking dead fish or seaweed off the beach.

Lake property is a lot of work. Aside from the things that had to be done, I tried not to create extra projects for myself. Our cabin was on almost an acre of land. Silently and profusely, I thanked God when we discovered that I was too short to reach the pedals on the riding lawn mower. The task of cutting the grass would fall to my husband or to our son. My love was the great indoors: knitting, reading, baking, cooking, or doing cross-stitch.

At the time, we had a rescued, multicolored Tortie cat named Shasta. Cuddly and serene in the confines of our home, the same cat was unrecognizable as she traveled proudly and purposefully out the back door of our cabin. Our snuggly Shasta became a mean, unmerciful hunting machine when she was released into the wild. It would not be unusual for me to drive into our yard and find a mangled body—lying limply on the back steps; a dead bird, a squirrel, or a chipmunk. I simply could not force myself to be an undertaker for these unfortunate creatures. If my son wasn't around to dispose of the victim, all I had to do was to walk next door and ask for help. Without hesitation, Sue came to my rescue. She never complained or criticized me for cowering out of sight until the thankless deed was completed.

One day, Sue and I were strolling along the lakeshore when a snake slithered slowly in front of us. Sue jumped away from the reptile and screamed as she recoiled in fear. Did I protect her or show any understanding for her phobia? No. Without thinking, I pretty much blew her off by saying, "Oh, Sue, it's just a little garter snake."

My friend was very quiet as we finished our walk. She was polite enough not to point out how thoughtless and insensitive I had been. Instead, she told me off in the very nicest way a few days later.

It was around two in the afternoon, our usual "Let's get together, chat, and drink coffee time," because we hadn't seen each other for three or four hours. I boosted myself onto one of her kitchen stools, and the chatting commenced.

After an hour of visiting and several cups of coffee, I got up and we said our good-byes. As I opened the door to leave, Sue softly remarked, "By the way, there's a dead bird lying on the path between our houses."

An expression of horror fell across my face. Then in an instant, I realized that there was no dead bird on the path. I had just been on that path. Sue was telling me as kindly as she could that she had taken care of me countless times, never once dismissing my fear. But I had betrayed her friendship by totally ignoring hers.

About a month later, Sue and I were clearing debris off the beach when a slippery little snake crawled out from underneath a rock near the place where we were working. A frightened look crossed Sue's face. Then sadly, she glanced in my direction to see if I was going to dismiss her feelings once again. Lesson learned, I sprinted as fast as I could, putting myself between her and the snake, until she could get a comfortable distance away from the shifty varmint.

The look of relief and gratitude on her face was all the thanks necessary, and I was grateful to God that there had been an opportunity to return, in a very small way, all the kindness my friend had generously shared with me so many times.

Sands of Time

"The goodness of God endureth continually." (Psalm 52:1)

Once in a while, something happens that takes our breath away. It startles, brings a tear—perhaps a smile.

After my mother's death a few years ago, my brothers, sister, and I gathered together to go through her belongings. If there was ever an amicable distribution of possessions, our family managed to achieve it. Among the treasures in my mother's cedar chest were three dolls. My sister Kay, who likes dolls, realized years ago when I tried to adopt—steal—all her babies, that I probably loved dolls more than she did. To me, dolls were real. They were my babies. To her, I suspect that a doll was only a toy. Imagine.

As Kay and I sat in front of Mother's old cedar chest, pulling one item out of it at a time, gazing, questioning what it might have meant to her, Kay graciously offered to give our mother's dolls to me. The tears that welled up in my eyes, and my hands cupped over my heart, seemed to convey all the gratitude necessary to my sister for her generous offer.

I don't believe the dolls had much monetary value. The backsides of the fragile rubber were deeply stamped with huge letters that read, "Made in Japan." One doll had a golden pageboy painted on her porcelain head, complete with a light, saucy blue ribbon off to one side. Her face was delicate and sweet. The second doll was much like the first, but didn't have the painted touches that the first doll was adorned with. Since my mother was born in 1918, I suspect that the dolls would have dated back to the 1920s.

The third doll was a slim, graceful geisha girl that my father brought back with him as a gift to our mother upon returning from his stint as an army medic during World War II. She sits on the top shelf of our bookcase. Her eyes gaze down from her perch with a peaceful, mystical expression on her pasty, white face. Her head lies to one side or the other in a horizontal position. She has been like that ever since I can remember. Every time I move her, I try to correct her unfortunate dilemma. Silly me. She is in need of professional help.

The two little dolls have found a home on the lower shelves of our bookcase, each leaning against a book in a sitting position for support.

As per tradition, something is always overlooked at our house when the Christmas adornments are tucked away for the season. As I dusted the bookshelf that hadn't been touched since the decorations landed on it three weeks before Christmas, there it was. The Precious Moments manger scene waiting patiently for its return to a storage box in anticipation of the next Christmas season.

Picking up the remnants of the daily newspaper, I rolled Joseph, Mary, baby Jesus, the wise men, donkeys, shepherds, and an assortment of little lambs into the morning edition. With great care, and a little reluctance, I carefully tucked the delicate pieces of the crèche into a box and delivered the holiday stragglers to their resting place in the basement. Then I returned to the bookcase and my dusting duties.

With rag in hand, freshly sprayed with Pledge, I picked up my mother's baby doll so that I could dust underneath her. As I did this, her leg dropped, and a few grains of sand slipped out, landing on the bookcase shelf. I gasped in surprise at what had just happened. My mother must have played with this toy in her sandbox at one time, and the sand had been inside that doll since my mother's childhood.

MARY EMERSON

It was such a small thing. A few minute grains of sand slipping from the body of a doll. With unforeseen tears and a smile, I stood in front of the bookcase holding a piece of my mother's long-gone-by childhood in my hands, and in my heart.

Why Do You Love Me?

"Thou art my Father, my God." (Psalm 89:26)

"Why do you love me?" God asked me one day.

Did I hear him correctly?

That's easy, I thought a little smugly to myself. Yet when I tried to find the words to explain my reason for loving him, I was surprised to discover how difficult it was to come up with an answer.

"Because you're God?" I answered lamely.

"Do you want me to love you because you're my daughter?"

Of course I wanted him to love me because I was his daughter. But I wanted more reason than "I have to love you because you're my daughter." Obviously, God was asking the same thing in reverse: "I have to love you because you're God?"

Throughout the day, the question pestered me, following me everywhere, gnawing at my thoughts with everything I did. As the minutes turned to hours, the struggle for an answer to God's seemingly easy question continued to be elusive. Frustrated, I shrugged my shoulders and humbly admitted defeat.

"What did you love about your father?" God asked me.

There were so many fond memories of the times that I had spent with my dad. He was always happy to see me when he came home from work. When I was a small child, he would throw me up in the air, swing me by one arm and one leg, with me pleading for him to "do it one more time, Dad." We listened to classical music together on Sunday afternoons, music that I hated at the time, but endured, because I loved just being with my father.

In the summertime, I would sit on the curb and wait at the street corner for his wobbly black pickup to rumble down the dusty, unpaved road toward me. With a wave of his hand and a foot on the brakes, he would stop and let me climb on to his lap. My tiny hands encircled the steering wheel, and with a smile of delight on my face, I would "drive" the half a block to our house. The driving was fun. But what was really special was the fact that my father had taken time out of his hectic day to spend with me.

Quite honestly, the question had been answered early on in the day. I love God because he is my Father. He is there for me, and hopefully, I am there for him. He gifts me his love without condition. He cares for me, and I love him back.

Love is what it is: a condition and the language of our heart.

Tomorrow Morning

"He hath shewed thee, O man, what is good: and what doeth the Lord require of thee, but to do justly, and to love mercy, and to walk humbly with our God." (Micah 6:8)

Even as a child I struggled with some of the things that Christ did in his ministry. For instance, it seemed curious to me the way he approached the matter of healing the blind, the deaf, and the crippled. Before granting their petition, Jesus often asked them, "Do you want to be healed?" If their answer was yes, he required them to do something odd, like putting mud or spit on their eyes or in their ears. Eww.

One day, I asked Jesus why he wanted to know from the person who was in need of his healing touch, if they, in fact, *wanted* to be healed. I mean, seriously? You have been blind, deaf, or lame all of your life, or most of your life. Then suddenly someone offers to change that for you. What's to think about?

"Well," Christ explained patiently. "I heal you, and you get your sight back, or your hearing. You can walk and run and jump. You go home to your family with the story of how you were touched by the Master, and now you are well. Your family is in awe when they see what has happened to you, and they throw a party to celebrate your great news. But what happens when the celebration is over?

"Tomorrow morning, you can't go and sit by the gate waiting for Omar or Martha or Paul to come by with money to throw into your basket so that you can exist. No one carries you to the places you can't get to on your own. The days of being taken care of by others are over. Tomorrow morning, you are just like everyone else. You have no education, you have no skills, and you can no longer live off of the kindness of other people. Tomorrow morning, you have to go out and find a job. And every morning after that, you have to find a way to support yourself."

The reality of how their life would change after being healed had never occurred to me.

"Soooo—why did you require them to do something that seemed ridiculous before you made them whole?"

Jesus smiled as he continued teaching his lesson. "I don't like being used any more than anyone else does. Did people want my touch so they could go on their way and forget about me? Or were they willing to humble themselves, obey me, and follow me?"

Obedience shows love and respect to our God, even though we don't always understand the requests he makes of us. Yet he always finds a way to reward and bless us when we honor him.

About the Author

Mary Emerson was born and raised in a small Northern Minnesota town. She and her husband, a retired vice president of a large corporation, have been married for forty-six years. God's grace has provided many unexpected blessings in their lives. Together, they have traveled to Europe, were honored to spend a night at an embassy party with friends, and entertained former governor Judy Martz and her cabinet in their home.

Mary began her writing career with the story "A Tap at the Window," which was published in the March 2014 issue of *Guidepost* magazine. Her greatest joy is spending time with her family, and the family of her heart, her friends.